Cisco,

Have No Fear. -

Dream Big - -

Enjoy

TRANSFORM YOUR LIFE AND FIND SUCCESS

LEADING FEARLESSLY

JORDAN ZIMMERMAN

GREENLEAF
BOOK GROUP PRESS

Published by Greenleaf Book Group Press
Austin, Texas
www.gbgpress.com

Copyright ©2015 Jordan Zimmerman & Zimmerman Advertising, LLC

Distributed by Greenleaf Book Group

For ordering information or special discounts for bulk purchases, please contact Greenleaf Book Group at PO Box 91869, Austin, TX 78709, 512.891.6100.

Design and composition by Greenleaf Book Group
Cover design by Greenleaf Book Group

Publisher's Cataloging Publication Data is available.

ISBN: 978-1-62634-163-0

Part of the Tree Neutral® program, which offsets the number of trees consumed in the production and printing of this book by taking proactive steps, such as planting trees in direct proportion to the number of trees used: www.treeneutral.com

TreeNeutral

Printed in the United States of America on acid-free paper

15 16 17 18 19 20   10 9 8 7 6 5 4 3 2 1

First Edition

Other Edition:
eBook ISBN: 978-1-62634-164-7

To the loving memory of my father, whose guidance, strength, and wisdom made me the man and leader that I am today.

CONTENTS

For More Information   ix

Introduction: You're reading this book because you're tired
   of your own bullshit.   1

PART I

BE LIKE ME, INSANELY COMMITTED
TO DOING WHATEVER IT TAKES

1   Be insanely committed to your own life.   9

2   Be insanely committed to what you know is right.   17

3   Be insanely committed to the suffering and the sacrifice.   27

4   Be insanely committed to being the best at whatever you
     choose to do.   37

5   Be insanely committed to competition.   45

6   Be insanely committed to your own professionalism.   59

7   Be insanely committed to the people who rely on you.   67

PART II

PRIDE, EXCUSES, AND LIES
YOU TELL YOURSELF

8 No excuses. 77

9 Quit being proud. No job is beneath you. 85

10 Life is unfair. Succeed anyway. 91

11 Attack of the bullshitters! 97

12 You can't build a better horse. 103

13 Doing brain surgery on yourself. 109

PART III

FAILURE, FEAR, AND FOULING UP

14 If you want somebody you can trust, trust yourself. 115

15 You, too, can fail like me! 119

16 Fear is fuel. 125

17 Screwing up and getting screwed over. 133

PART IV

THE TROPHY GENERATION VERSUS
PEOPLE WHO ACTUALLY DO THINGS

18 Giving everybody a trophy doesn't create winners. It just
    makes more losers. 143

19 Quit being an entitled little prince or princess from the
    Trophy Generation and embrace reality. 149

20 The inspiration of desperation. 155

CONTENTS

PART V

THERE'S ONLY ONE FINISH LINE— DON'T LOSE SIGHT OF IT

21 Outcome beats output every single time.   165

22 Toothless lions.   173

23 If you want to build a railroad, sometimes you have to build a steel mill first.   181

24 Will the real Jordan Zimmerman please stand up?   193

PART VI

START MAKING PROGRESS TODAY, NOT TOMORROW

25 If you don't have a goal, you don't have a life.   203

26 Find the real problem.   209

27 Get an education, or get a broom.   223

28 Did I hurt your feelings? You're welcome.   231

29 How *not* to live your life *or* leading fearlessly versus following fearfully.   237

30 The sayings of Chairman Z.   247

Index   257

About the Author   267

For More Information

www.zadv.com

Twitter: @jzspeaks

www.yousleepwhenyoudie.com

www.jzleadingfearlessly.com

Facebook: Jordan Zimmerman

YOU'RE READING THIS BOOK BECAUSE YOU'RE TIRED OF YOUR OWN BULLSHIT.

INTRODUCTION

Do you want it or not?

I don't care what it is—a job, a career, a lifestyle, a level of success, whatever. Do you really want it? Because if you don't have it right now, today, it's your fault and no one else's.

Don't give in to excuses about who or what stopped you or how you had some obligation that got in your way. The fact is you chose something other than your dream. Every excuse is bullshit. Every. Single. One.

This doesn't make you a *bad person, but it ought to make you an aware person—aware that what has happened so far in your life has been entirely up to you.*

And aware that what happens next, for good or bad, is also in your hands.

Life is a series of choices. For each one, you can choose to sacrifice toward your goal or to accept short-term gratification. Think of the first big decision that many people make, going to college. You may have to live on almost nothing for four years and borrow a lot of money—that is, you'll make a sacrifice—as a trade for something of greater value, an education that will open doors and serve you well for the rest of your life. More choices will follow: Are you the guy who's out the door at five o'clock, or are you the one who stays late to do more? Are you the one who opens the new branch, or the one who is just happy to work there? Are you the secretary who leaves to start her own business, or are you satisfied to get a paycheck for simply showing up?

Every day you make a choice to move closer to doing the thing you love or moving away from it. You're reading this because you've realized that you really do want something out there more than you want what you have and that you are going to take the first step to get it.

Congratulations, because in that realization lies a

deep truth and a bold opportunity: There's not a thing in the world you can't achieve *if* you are willing to work hard to get it. It won't be easy. You'll have to strive for clarity of mind, sweat for strength of body, and exhaust your energy for commitment to purpose. These are not just words. You're about to take the first step on a path that's a way of life. I know it works because I did it, and I do it every day. I've taught others to do it. Real achievers were doing it long before I came along.

No matter when you get started, you can always get what you want. It's never too late to begin, never too late to turn things around. *Never.* Don't let time be yet another excuse.

So now you know why you're reading this book: You're tired of your own bullshit. There's something you want to do. It's the thing you love, and you're tired of hearing excuses in your head that you can't or won't refute. Go ahead, rattle them off right now:

I need the security of the job I already have.
I'm afraid to risk what I've earned so far.
Times are tough; I'd be foolish to bail on a good thing.
I have a good enough life already.

And then there's the worst one of all:

It probably wouldn't have worked out anyway.

Enough. You either seize the opportunity, or you don't.

Since you've read this far, I'm going to assume that you're ready—really ready—to take control of your career and your life and go after your dream.

I'm going to show you the way.

There are specific steps you're going to have to take. Each step will require you to do some things you're not in the habit of doing. Uncomfortable things. You'll have to choose sacrifice over short-term gain. You'll have to build your body, hone your mind, and strengthen your will. You're *not* going to forsake your obligations. Instead, you're going to figure out which obligations are real and which are just in your head, and then you're going to meet them *while* you pursue your new goal. And you're going to find the energy to do all this—energy that right now you can't imagine having.

I'll show you how to do all that.

So take the first step. Since life is a series of choices, make your first one, maybe one of the first conscious, purposeful decisions you've ever made: Go down the path that leads to what you really want. No matter the pain. No matter the effort. No matter the loss of the materially comfortable corner you've made for yourself. You think this is about money? This is about your life.

And if you don't choose to pursue the things you say you love, you can be sure that you didn't love them in the first place.

Today I choose to begin. Say it out loud. Write it on a piece of paper, and place it where you can see it. Stick it on your mirror. Put it on all your doors. Remind yourself of it every hour. This isn't a gimmick. This is the creation of a habit: You have to establish your goal in your mind so that it's there with every choice you make. Those choices—easy or hard, closer to the goal or further away—will come along all the time. But from now on you're going to recognize them as they appear. And the choices you make now will be very different from the choices you made before.

Life is too important to waste, and your time is too short.

Congratulations, and welcome to the club.

PART I

BE LIKE ME, INSANELY COMMITTED TO DOING WHATEVER IT TAKES

BE INSANELY COMMITTED TO YOUR OWN LIFE.

I want to let you in on one of my deepest, darkest secrets: I am insane.

I promise that after you read this book, you are going to want to adopt my insanity, because it works—especially for people like you, who want to achieve a dream and who are willing to do whatever it takes to get it.

Was I born insane? It might be part of my DNA, but it also has something to do with where I grew up. Every day I saw a lot of unhappy people—my parents' friends and my friends' parents—going to jobs that they didn't like to pay for things they didn't need in pursuit of a dream they couldn't name. I said that when I grew up, there was no way I'd be like them. I would live out my passion through the work that I chose. I would go to work every day to have the greatest time in the world.

And today? That's what I do.

When I was young, one of my first jobs was delivering newspapers. A lot of great entrepreneurs begin with basic jobs like that. My paper route started with sixty-two homes. But when I realized there were 4,400 homes in my neighborhood, I said to myself, *Here's an opportunity! How big do I want this to be?* Before I knew it, I had 460 homes.

I was sneaking out of the house at 2:30 one morning to deliver my papers—I had to get started that early to complete my route before school—and I ran into my mother. "Where are you going?" she said. "To deliver my papers!" I answered. She looked at me and said, "Son, are you insane? It's 2:30 in the morning, and this is the last day you are delivering papers at 2:30 a.m.!"

So a few hours later I went to school with a problem, but I came home with a solution: I hired two friends to work with me. I had just promoted myself from paperboy to paperboy manager!

I had to learn how to inspire my new "employees." Fortunately, I had a great mentor. My grandfather owned a bottling plant in northern New Jersey that produced syrups, toppings, and colas. He told me, "You need to be insanely committed to the kind of products you put out. You need to be insanely committed to your customers, so much so that you need to figure out how to be available all day, every day. You need to be insanely committed to the great employees you have. And you need to be insanely committed to your own life."

I applied his advice to every aspect of my life, and I've lived by those rules ever since. In fact, on the back of my business card, and that of every Zimmerman associate, you'll find this: "24/7 (Seriously)."

In my senior year at the University of South Florida (USF), I had an opportunity to put my insane commitment into practice. I was offered a slot in the most important competition I could imagine, more important than any high school football game. This was a real step on the ladder of life.

The National Institute on Drug Abuse (NIDA) was tasked with helping to end drug abuse among the youth of America. They held a contest among advertising and marketing majors in college. The challenge was to create a campaign they could use around the nation—something that would be memorable, compelling, and potentially game changing.

My team and I took on that challenge with an insane commitment to winning and with the firm belief that in life there is no second place.

Competing against every college and university in the country, our USF team won.

After our triumph, we went to Washington, DC, for ceremonies and meetings in the White House. We presented our campaign to the vice president, the first lady, the head of NIDA, and fifty other government figures. It was an amazing day, one I can never forget. It was the first time in my adult life that I saw what's possible if you have an insane commitment to your own goals and your own life.

As for that campaign we produced? Whether you're from the United States or the other side of the world, I'm sure you've heard of it. You may have even grown up with it.

Our winning slogan was "Just Say No."

Not long after, I took that campaign—and my brand-new diploma—to New York City, where I made ten appointments for job interviews with the most prestigious advertising firms on Madison Avenue.

I came out of those meetings zero for ten.

Can you imagine how that felt? As a college student, I had helped create one of the most recognizable slogans and memorable campaigns of the twentieth century, yet these guys couldn't see my obvious genius!

It turned out that at this point in my life, I wasn't the genius I thought I was. Still, I thought to myself, *How dare they*? I had accomplished more before the age of twenty-one than most of these men and women would in their entire careers. And they had the gall to tell me no?

I had dreamed of working on Madison Avenue, and just like that, these folks in suits and ties were denying me my goal.

A lot of people would have given up. You know, you get the rarest of opportunities—to make a personal pitch to the people in the corner office at the prestigious place you imagined yourself working—and your very best idea gets shot out of the sky.

Most people would have said that if "Just Say No" doesn't impress them, nothing ever will. Normal people would get rejected and give up. But I'm not normal. I'm insane, remember?

My reaction was exactly the opposite of normal: *No! I don't care who you are or how much you know. I'm not allowing you to rob me of my dream. You can't make me give it up, and you can't take it away.*

I was angry and hurt, but I wasn't going to cut off my nose to spite my face. If these were the guys I needed to impress, I had to know what it would take to get their attention. And once I cooled off, I realized they had already told me. At every appointment, I heard the same appraisal: *You need more education.* I grabbed on to that like a life preserver and made more education my new, intermediate goal, believing that it would help me get to my big goal. I erased the bitterness, every bit of it. It was forgotten—so long, the end. I wasn't going to let any naysayer live rent-free in my head. I was going to spend my energy taking productive action on my insane commitment, not on nursing hurt feelings.

I had always valued education, because it seemed like the way to get ahead. Now I was experiencing that truth firsthand. The only way I was going to make it into that big advertising world was through more education.

If I ever thought I knew it all, those Madison Avenue executives helped me knock that idea out of my head. Evidently I lacked a few key skills. Coming up with a great campaign wasn't all it would take to succeed in marketing and advertising. In my case, I needed to go to business school.

Not everybody needs an advanced degree in order to succeed. You, for instance, may not need one. But at that point in my life, I had to know what a business school graduate knows, so back to USF I went!

Surprises were in store there too. On the first day of my first class, I responded to my professor's lecture by telling him not only that he was wrong but also that the textbook was wrong. He stared back at me, a first-year, first-day loudmouth—an insane kid standing alone in the middle of that huge classroom—and he said . . .

Well, you'll have to keep reading this book to find out.

The first lesson for you is this: Be insanely committed to your own life. Be dedicated, committed, unrelenting, unfailing, and unstoppable. In every impossible moment there is great opportunity, but the only people who figure that out are the ones willing to bust their ass to find it, to persevere, to work past the point when everyone else has packed it in.

Be insanely committed to your own life. Never give up!

JZ's CHAPTER TIPS

» Find your passion.

» Work doesn't feel like work when you love the work you do.

» Be insanely committed to your work, no matter what.

» Don't let a naysayer live rent-free in your head.

» Never quit.

BE INSANELY COMMITTED TO WHAT YOU KNOW IS RIGHT.

CHAPTER 2

After I graduated from college, helped create one of the most remembered ad campaigns in history, and then was shot down by the top advertising agencies on Madison Avenue, my insane commitment was as strong as ever, but I had been humbled. I returned to the University of South Florida's business school ready to listen and learn. My experience had made me aware of where I was deficient: I needed more managerial ability, greater knowledge about finance, and a deeper understanding of marketing. So one more time, I enrolled, showed up, shut my mouth, and prepared to be educated.

But nothing ever goes as planned, especially when you're insane. I quickly realized that I was going to have to learn another kind of insanity: the insane commitment to what you know is right, even when you feel like you're the only one who "gets it."

My first class was in marketing—how to promote the things you want to sell. It wouldn't be long before I figured out that my professor, Dr. Stephens, was a bona fide genius. In only a few short months he would become a mentor to me. But that day he was just the first face I saw in front of the chalkboard.

On my initial day in his class, he showed us something called a purchase funnel, which is academic jargon for something you don't need to completely understand. Basically the funnel shows that the first step to success—at the wide end—is making people aware of your product. The next step is getting them to choose your product over the alternatives. The last step, at the narrow point, is making a profit.

As you have already figured out, when I sense something that's off, I call it that way. If that makes trouble, I don't care, even if I get caught in the middle. I am insanely committed to the truth, whatever it is and wherever it leads, and this drawing on the board was definitely not right. I can't imagine how it made sense to anyone who had actually succeeded in business! Perhaps using more colorful language than I should have, I said, "What? The last step is to work on profit? Are you serious? What the hell are we in business for, to be popular? Maybe we get lucky and make a dime or two in the end?"

The allegedly brilliant insight of the funnel—*work on popularity before you work on profit*—was being offered as the foundation of an education I had been told was vital, yet this foundational idea was in complete and utter opposition to everything I had seen in real life, from my family's businesses to my own success as a young entrepreneur. I had just one reaction: *You have to be kidding me.*

There's no school like experience. I had already learned a few things about business from my grandfather, who had become successful at it long before I was born. He had shown me the ropes at an early age—not just how the business worked but also why. By the time I walked into that classroom, I had been around enough companies to know what works and what doesn't. Every single business plan I had ever seen was a detailed map focused on becoming more profitable. Nothing else could possibly make sense to anybody who had set foot in the real world.

So I said to my distinguished professor, "Hey, boss. Your funnel is upside down. *Profitability* goes on top! Come on, we all know that! A brand that's profitable has revenue. A brand that's profitable has margins. A brand that's profitable has market share."

I was already in deep, so I figured I might as well finish the point. As the rest of the class waited for Dr. Stephens to flunk me on the spot, I refuted the funnel according to the truth I knew: You can't build a business unless you figure out how to make money. I said that when a brand turns a profit, then all the other parts of the funnel before the purchase—awareness, opinion, consideration, and preference—all that happens naturally. To sustain a business, your goal *must* be to earn a profit. If you can't do that, you can't pay the bills, and your business won't last anyway. There's only one pathway leading to a viable business. It's called commitment to profit, and it requires hard work.

So I finished sharing my point of view, and then I realized what I had done: A first-day-of-the-first-year student had just taken on a professor in front of the whole class! Was I insane?

Yeah, I was. Just like today.

In that moment, as I realized what could happen to my grad-school career, I prepared myself for the consequences. *Stand by for the storm.* In my mind, I was already packing my bags.

But you know what? Even with that possibility in front of me, I did not hesitate. I was standing up for the truth as I saw it, so I didn't care. The truth is always going to be the truth, no matter who doesn't like it.

Then Dr. Stephens proved why he was such a good professor: He considered what I had said, paused, and no, he didn't throw me out on my ass. Just the opposite! Instead, he told me that I was onto something. He said, I should keep analyzing, examining, and questioning like that all semester—and for the rest of my career in business.

He could have dressed me down in front of everybody and told me to hit the road, but he didn't. He told me to keep thinking for myself.

That was a hell of a discovery: Here was a man who was just as committed to the truth as I was! He didn't worry about getting credit for being right. All he wanted was to become better and smarter at what he did, so he could put it to use.

I could identify with him. He questioned everything, and he would hear anybody out, even a kid with
attitude. If you're insanely committed to the truth, you
don't care where the truth comes from, a PhD or a kid
in his first day of class. You never know where the
next idea is going to spring from, so you have to keep
your mind open.

I took Dr. Stephens' good advice. I kept listening to
my professors every day, analyzing and questioning. It
paid off too—and not just for me. Not only did I get
the education I needed, two decades later I endowed
the Zimmerman Advertising Program (ZAP) at USF. It's
an interdisciplinary program that provides an education in advertising unlike any in the world. I created
it, and continue to support it, so that young people
can be taught the rigorous logic, discipline, and tech-
nical skills that the real world demands. ZAP leaves in
the dust advertising professionals who think they can
substitute smooth talk and a shoeshine for the hard
work of analytical thinking and metrics.

That first day was my most important day at business school because it set the course for my life. I
had just heard that not everybody was putting profit
first—at least not the guys writing b-school textbooks.

Experts could be wrong! It seemed like I was the only guy who had figured that out, and many times it still seems like that.

But now you know it too.

I realized that the most obvious truth of business—that you make money by giving people what they need, not by blindly following what's expected—is not so clear to everyone. Some people focus on tactics and the path right in front of them, while the best of us focus relentlessly on the big goal, the greater truth, the point down the road that we are determined to reach.

I knew what I wanted to achieve, and I had suddenly gained a better idea of how to get there.

The gears started spinning in my head, and that night sleep wasn't on the agenda. I don't sleep much anyway—you can sleep when you die—and I spent the night awake, hunched over my desk, and killing cup after cup of coffee. By the morning I had the first draft of a business plan for something no one had created before: an advertising agency built solely on client success. Screw the distraction of output; by that I meant we would not worry about impressing our competitors or winning awards for fancy commercials. We would focus relentlessly on creating profitable, positive, business-boosting, bottom-line-building outcomes for our clients. Instead of selling promises, we would sell results!

At that time, ad agencies were not results driven. But we would be.

Ad agencies were not customer focused. But we would be.

And agencies certainly were not measuring their results. But we would do that.

I was going to build the first advertising agency that provided a comprehensive response to a client's needs. I would build an advertising agency concerned with more than just advertising. I would build a *business solutions firm*, the first of its kind, and it would be driven by metrics—that is, we would measure our successes in concrete terms that would leave no doubt as to whether we had delivered on our promises.

We would take on the problems of our clients' businesses, whatever those problems were. Advertising would be the industry we worked in, but our product would be success.

We would succeed only when our client succeeded. That was the ultimate incentive. The client's needs would become our needs.

In only a few years, after I had put my business plan into action, we became a multimillion-dollar success by putting clients ahead of everything.

It all started because Jordan Zimmerman was and still is so insane that he believes in the truth no matter who says something different and no matter where it leads.

As for you, here's my advice: Be insane. Believe what you know is true. Don't let anybody throw you off course.

JZ's CHAPTER TIPS

» If you're insanely committed to the truth, you don't care where it comes from, a PhD or a student on his first day of class.

» The truth is always the truth, no matter who doesn't like it or who tells you otherwise.

» Keep questioning.

» Smooth talk and a shoeshine are no substitute for the hard work of analytical thinking and metrics.

» You succeed by giving people what they need, not by blindly following what's expected.

» Make your client's needs your own needs.

» You sleep when you die.

BE INSANELY COMMITTED TO THE SUFFERING AND THE SACRIFICE.

CHAPTER 3

It's one thing to be insanely committed to *doing* something. It's another thing to be insanely committed to tolerating what the world does to you. I was about to learn a third kind of insane commitment: suffering for your goal and sacrificing to get there.

Two years earlier the New York ad men wouldn't let me in the front door of their castle, so I decided to build my own.

On my first day at business school, I identified the goal for my professional life and the outline of a plan to get there: When I graduated, I would open the world's first client-centered business solutions firm that happened to do advertising. This company would be metrics driven, which, in turn, would drive profits for our clients. My firm would focus solely on **building profits** for our clients—and we would not worry about winning recognition for ourselves. If we took care of the people who relied on us, all the other trappings of success would come our way without asking. I knew it would be a success for two reasons:

1 Failure was not an option.

2 No one else in the advertising industry had yet been smart enough to stop worrying about winning awards for their artsy TV commercials and start focusing exclusively on the success of the client.

At the time client-centered focus sounded insane. But I am insane enough to walk through hell to accomplish whatever I dream up.

Not long after I had graduated from business school, I opened that agency. Let me tell you about it: Close your eyes and picture a dump.

Now imagine living next door to that dump and wishing your own place was as nice.

That's where I set up shop, next to a dump.

You think I'm kidding? I'm not. Here it is.

Zimmerman Advertising began behind the trash pile at the crappiest end of the crappiest strip mall in the crappiest neighborhood you can imagine. To get to the front door of my office, you had to walk around a seven-foot-high dumpster, but at least it was my office. *Mine*. It was the first incarnation of my dream.

Was it a pleasant place for an office? Of course not. Was it where I wanted to be forever? No way! But if you really want to achieve your dream, you have to be willing to suffer and sacrifice to get it. The fact is, for someone right out of business school, that little hole in the wall was exactly where I needed to be.

I fought through any doubts with this truth: *Success isn't about where you start out. It's where you're going and what you're willing to sacrifice to get there.*

I was ready to sacrifice. I was there to build my business. I was there to grow. I was there to learn. I was going to search out clients, perfect my approach, and turn the advertising world upside down by serving clients better than anyone else ever had!

Those Madison Avenue guys were going to wonder how some upstart kid in South Florida had managed to drive up the bottom line of his own clients in ways the New York boys had never imagined.

It was going to demand sacrifice.

And that crappy office space was just one little part of what I was willing to put up with in order to achieve my dream.

By day I worked in a dump. At night I went home to my parents' house. For six years I spent my nights on a foldout couch in a spare room they let me have for nothing.

I could have rented a place of my own, could have made it nice, and believe me, I wanted that. But I wanted something else even more: I wanted success in my business and in my life. I didn't have the money, time, or resources to live high on the hog and work toward my dream at the same time. There wouldn't be enough money for both, and I didn't intend to spend any more of my mental energy than I had to on food and four walls.

I poured all my earnings back into my new firm. Every day, every minute, every hour. No matter how much money I made, I sacrificed so I could invest in technology and people. While my friends went out for a nice dinner, I became the master of the can opener. I drove a clunker—a gold 1973 Montego. I wore old clothes. I didn't splurge on movies or trips or impressing a girlfriend. I had the self-discipline to sacrifice for my dream.

It wasn't as bad as I'm making it sound. Not for me. *Why? I love the work.* Loved it then, love it now. The truth is that I didn't really care about having a polo player on the front of my shirt or a Nike swoosh on my sneakers. My dreams were bigger than just material things, and they still are today. My greatest dream was and is achievement, pure and simple.

But to achieve a dream tomorrow, you have to do without things today.

If you're looking for a mantra to keep in your mind

on this journey—something to help keep you on track when the temptations to do something easier get to you—think of that simple idea, and say it to yourself: *I'm going without today for the bigger win tomorrow.*

Many of you might not believe you can handle that kind of sacrifice. Well, surprise! Every single one of you can, whether you think you're capable of it or not.

Each of you reading this book can make that sacrifice, but not all of you will. It's not a question of ability. It's a question of choice.

If you don't choose to succeed, you're choosing to fail. It's your call.

You're going to spend your life on one thing: what you choose to make important. Some choose immediate self-gratification. They settle for what's in front of them and call it good enough. Others of us dream a lot bigger than dinner menus and designer shirts or ski boats and beach houses. We want to stretch our abilities, make our mark, change the world, transform our dreams into reality. We want to achieve, achieve, achieve.

When you look at life that way, sacrifice and suffering don't seem so hard. In fact, they seem like the obvious choice.

The truth is that if you dream big enough, the trappings of success will naturally follow. And the rewards you will want may very well change along the way.

Most people don't want to put in the time or the energy to sacrifice for greatness in their life, but sacrifice is exactly what's required. Your sacrifice will pay off. Mine has paid off for me. If you're ever near Fort Lauderdale, swing by 3074 NW 60th Avenue, in Sunrise, and take a look. Unless somebody has bought that property and rebuilt it by the time you get there—maybe in pursuit of his own dream—it's still a pretty ragged corner. That's where my first office was and where I pursued my own dream for six long, difficult, sacrifice-filled, glorious years. Take a picture of it in your mind, and keep driving. I have another place for you to look at too.

We've moved a few times since then. Success has a way of doing that to you. Just recently, we moved into our new corporate headquarters: five stories of concrete, steel, and glass, more than twice the size of the 65,000-square-foot space we were in before. Think of it: from 400 square feet in the corner of a strip mall in a sketchy neighborhood long ago to 130,000 square feet all to ourselves in a thriving area. We now occupy the most innovative and inspirational advertising agency office space in the world. This architectural representation of excellence is a South Florida landmark.

I imagine we'll outgrow this one too. I could tell you that I hope so, but I don't have to hope. I expect it.

Not for a single minute have I ever been content to simply sit back and enjoy things the way they are. If you have energy in your body and air in your lungs, why the hell would you waste any of it? I'm always dreaming, always planning, always executing, always achieving. And I'll keep sacrificing. Because when you dream big, dare to fail, and learn the value of sacrifice, anything is possible.

JZ's CHAPTER TIPS

» If you are not choosing to succeed, you are choosing to fail.

» Work toward your dreams, not your rewards.

» Dream big. Dare to fail. Learn the value of sacrifice.

» To achieve your dreams tomorrow, do without today.

BE INSANELY COMMITTED TO BEING THE BEST AT WHATEVER YOU CHOOSE TO DO.

CHAPTER 4

I've talked about insane commitment to your own life, to what you know is true, and to the suffering and sacrifice that all successful people experience. But having all that commitment and expecting to succeed at your goal is pretty much the same as being the king of the gym and expecting to succeed at football.

A football player has to be very good at football! And whatever you want to do—own a business, be promoted to manager, become a dental hygienist, build a log cabin for your vacation in the mountains— you have to master the skills that are required. Some you can learn in school, some you learn on the job, some just come with experience, but however they come, you'll have to have an insane commitment to being the best.

People ask me lots of questions about my life. That's fine. I like talking about myself! People often ask me how I became successful and how they can become successful too: "What's one thing I can start doing right now to achieve my dreams?"

That's the point of my book and a question I am obviously happy to answer.

But first, a question of my own: *Out of all the other advertising agencies in America and the world, why do you think clients choose Zimmerman? There are hundreds of other agencies, several bigger and better known than mine. So what's the reason to call me instead of them?*

The answer is that I give clients something no other agency can or will. We have special skills that are vanishingly hard to find—so hard to find, in fact, that no one in this industry has them but us. Plus, we are the best at what we do.

Let me explain. Some agencies treat the advertising business like a Hollywood movie, shot on somebody else's dime. They sit around a $100,000 conference table and talk about whether the commercial was funny enough or clever enough and whether it would be "the one" to propel someone's advertising career into the stratosphere.

Not at Zimmerman.

If you're going to overdo things, don't overdo it on gloss that merely makes the agency look good. Overdo it on what matters to the client: success.

At Zimmerman, we have never, not for a second, been focused on bringing glory to ourselves. We're focused 100 percent on the client. When people hire us, we go in and learn how their business works from the inside out. We figure out what clients need in order to add to their bottom line. They hired us to help them make more money, so that's what we do. We're not about pretty promises and self-congratulations. We're about doing what we say we'll do for the people who depend on us.

I have the daily comps and transactions of my clients on my desk every morning. I review the clients' profit and loss sheets everyday. This is precisely why they hire Zimmerman: They know that what matters is not the *output* but rather the *outcome*—the money they take to the bank.

The world's most successful businesses (and those

that want to be) choose me over the rest: A.C. Moore, AutoNation, Ashley Furniture, Boston Market, CBS, Dunkin' Donuts, Extended Stay America, Firehouse Subs, the Florida Panthers, h.h. gregg, Lane Bryant, Logan's Roadhouse, Nissan, Office Depot, Papa John's, Party City, Tire Kingdom, White Castle, and many more. They know that out of all the agencies they could call, there's only one that does business the way I do it. We don't do advertising for the sake of output. We do advertising to create outcome.

I am acutely aware of the difference, and you should be too. Output versus outcome: What you produce on the way to the goal versus the goal itself.

Output can quickly turn into busywork, and a lot of the time, it is just that: projects and reports designed to make you look busy when the client wants to know what you're doing. But outcome—well, my clients never have to ask about outcome. I never hear *what's the point of all this?* All my clients have to do is look at their own bottom line before they came to Zimmerman Advertising and after.

We're in business to make each client's business more profitable.

We provide measurable results, and we care about

how things come out for the people paying us to work for them. These clients know we can do something for them that nobody else can, and what we do is help them dominate the market for the categories in which they are competing. What distinguishes Zimmerman from all the rest? We are committed to being the very best at what we do.

I know what I'm good at. I know what I have to offer the world. I know why I'm in demand. And I know the value of my expertise.

Now ask yourself, *Why would somebody come to me for help?* What expertise or special skills do I have that nobody else has? Identify your own strengths, and then work relentlessly toward perfecting them.

This may turn out to be demanding and difficult. But just because something's difficult doesn't mean you can skip doing it. You can do anything in the world that you set your mind to, you just have to keep working hard at it, maybe harder than anybody else. You will probably have to ask for help. Fine. That way it gets done.

Reaching the goal is a matter of will. Decide to do it—then do it, whatever it is. And do whatever it takes to be the best. There's plenty of room at the top, and plenty of business to go around once you get there. But you have to get there.

So back to the original question: What can you do right now, today, to get started on the road to your dream?

Be the best at what you do, and set yourself apart by your unique expertise and skills.

Ask yourself what you can provide to people that no one else can. If other people can do it, too, what distinguishes you from those other people? What makes you not just different but better? Constantly add to the list of things that distinguish you in a positive way from all the rest. Never stop improving the quality of what you do.

No matter what you want to do with your life and career, whether it's moving up to management, starting your own business, or building the biggest and best of anything, that will happen only if you distinguish yourself with an insane commitment to being the very best at it. If you set yourself apart in this way, then you give the world a reason to say, *That one over there, that's the person I want on my side. I can count on him. She's totally committed to getting this job done.*

He's insanely committed to being the best.

JZ's CHAPTER TIPS

» Master the skills that are necessary for you to achieve your goal.

» Provide measureable results.

» Constantly improve the quality of what you do.

» Reaching your goal is a matter of willpower.

BE INSANELY COMMITTED TO COMPETITION.

CHAPTER 5

Do you take care of your body? You should. I take care of mine. I've been at the gym almost every day since the early 1970s. I lift weights, I do cardio, I run; I have a regimen that I follow to keep me in as good or better shape than when I was in college. I have found that a strong body and a strong mind support each other. In fact, I believe it's hard to truly have one without the other.

But here's what I really want to tell you about. That daily workout to make my body stronger isn't enough by itself to keep me in the very best shape. I do something else, and anyone who's serious about his or her body does it too. Next time you're at the gym (and if you're not going already, you had better start), pick out the most in-shape men and women, and watch them. You'll see that while they're doing whatever they're doing, they're keeping an eye on somebody else who's doing it too.

And the one you're watching will beat that other person. They'll put in a few more sit-ups. A couple extra push-ups. An extra dozen crunches. Another round of reps. One more mile.

Why? They know that in order for them to improve their body, exercise isn't enough by itself. They need someone to push them. Someone to compete against. You need someone to drive you to do more.

We can't help it. It's human nature. We naturally want to compare our achievements to those of the people around us. And that's a good thing, because it helps us get better—faster, more skilled, more adept—at the things we do.

Competition pays off in improvement, victory, and success, and throughout most of the history of America, everybody understood it: Winners were recognized for talent and effort. Losers were motivated to try harder next time. Aside from some bruised egos, no one felt unimportant or unlikeable because of the experience.

As kids, we knew that our low-stakes competition was practice for important contests as adults. Do you remember playing outside with other kids in the neighborhood? I do. We had all kinds of games. We played touch football. We played stickball. We even played games we made up names for, like "Hot Beans" and "Ring-a-Lario." We played as hard as we could until we couldn't go anymore.

I don't recall who won most of those games; I just remember that we had fun. Over time I realized that we were learning to get along in competition and to organize ourselves toward a goal. That in turn made us closer friends and taught us how to improve our skills and, ultimately, ourselves.

What held us together? Competition, with a couple of ancient, dust-covered notions: self-discipline and sportsmanship.

Competition makes us better individuals and stronger, more cooperative, and happier members of a community. The purpose of competition is not to tear other people down but rather to cultivate the best in us. Competition quickly and efficiently shows us what we are good at and where we need to improve. Moreover, it also shows us the value of teamwork. The satisfaction we take from working together with something at stake is far greater than the increase in self-esteem that the "experts" promise when we pretend that everyone's a winner.

Today few people can say "competition" without choking on the word. Too many folks wrongly believe that competition amounts to pitting people against each other as personal enemies. Those people are wrong.

I'm disgusted by how far society has strayed from common sense. Competition is the way that civilized human beings motivate themselves to improve. And it is the foundation of the most successful economic system the world has ever seen, free enterprise. To denigrate competition is to deny society one of the great engines of progress.

Success is driven by competition, and competition is the key to quality. Competition is like the whetstone used to sharpen a knife: The friction makes the blade sharper. Competition is a great thing. That's a message you don't hear these days, and that's how we've ended up in a society up to the eyeballs in politically correct nonsense.

Competition is essential to success in life, and if you want to achieve your dreams, you're going to have to learn it and live it. Competition teaches us that the best and most important things—the accomplishments that make life better for us and others—come when people push themselves harder and stretch themselves beyond the point they would ordinarily go.

It's shortsighted and self-destructive to discount the value of competition. We need each other as competitors! The next time you watch a track meet and see the runners super close at the finish line, ask yourself this: Would the winner have run so fast or had such a great time if all those other runners weren't right behind, motivating him to go a little faster? It's the same thing in business. The constant competition from my peers keeps me searching every day to find better ways to serve my customers, to produce higher quality results, and to generate greater profits for the clients who depend on me. So I thank God for my competitors. Without them, I wouldn't have that impetus to do even more.

Let me take this one step further. Not only is competition necessary for excellence, it's required to achieve the most basic, acceptable quality.

For example, do you dread a visit to the Department of Motor Vehicles as much as I do? There's not much worse than wasting a day at the DMV, sitting in the waiting room, hoping for your number to be called. When you finally get to the window, you're often face to face with someone who is not exactly the friendliest or most competent person in the world. And if all your paperwork isn't ready, heaven help you, because you're going to get a sneer and a trip to the back of the line.

Why is that?

Because the DMV has zero competition. It's the only game in town. If you want to register your vehicle or renew your license, you have to go there. No other place can do it.

They don't treat you right because they don't have to. You can't do everything online with the DMV, and you can't cross the street to some other DMV. There's only one Department of Motor Vehicles, and the state runs it. The motto may as well be "My way, or you can't get on the highway."

I promise you, you won't get that kind of treatment anywhere else—at least not for long. Look down the road at the nearest fast-food place. If you walk in the front door and the food is lousy or the clerk at the counter gives you attitude, the owner knows that you'll go to some other fast-food joint where they do things better, and you'll never walk in his door again. That's why the fast-food entrepreneurs who succeed are obsessed with customer service and quality: They have to compete with lots and lots of other places. Customers have a choice.

In the fast-food business, competition keeps up the quality as well as the innovation. Ever wonder why all these places sell salads now? *The customers asked for them.* And every owner knew that if he didn't roll out healthier choices, his customers would patronize a place that did.

Compare that to the DMV. No competition means no incentive for quality. They don't care if you wait five minutes or five hours. They don't even have to do the job right, let alone well. Where else are you going to go?

Another great example of "We Don't Care Because We Don't Have To" is the United States Postal Service.

There is no bigger example of a waste-your-time, we-don't-care operation still in business.

Every few months I read that the post office is running out of money. (Maybe the check's in the mail, and they just haven't delivered it to themselves. Ha!) Here's my suggestion for cutting costs: Replace all those electric clocks with calendars. After all, they're not getting anything done that you can time with a minute hand. I've stood in line so long in my post office that I've celebrated a birthday in line. No wonder they tell you to mail your packages early for Christmas. You could spend days just getting to the counter. Say "post office" and what comes to mind? Service as fast as a crippled snail on a glacier.

Now the post office has competition. If you want something delivered on time and guaranteed to get there, you can go to FedEx. Take your package to Fred Smith's company, and it's a done deal.

So how does the post office survive? It's protected by the government; its existence is enshrined in the Constitution. (Which is a story in itself: The Founding Fathers wanted to guarantee delivery of messages to everyone, but they didn't anticipate that highways and technology would come along to open the business to other providers.) The post office has a permanent subsidy, no matter how bad things get for the people they serve.

When it really counts, which organization do you trust, the one who doesn't answer to anyone or the one who answers to you? Who would you rather have doing a job, the company that's going to survive whether it serves you well or not, or the company that does quality work?

Competition makes the difference. That's why I don't believe that people who complain about it and about free enterprise have what it takes to be successful entrepreneurs.

Fortunately, few businesses enjoy the luxury of being the only game in town or being subsidized and mandated by the U.S. government. The rest of us are up against people with goals and dreams much like our own, and that means if we want to be the winner, we have to be the best. Why do I say, "fortunately"? Because the path to success is a highway of competition, and that's good.

I doubt you've heard anyone praise competition recently. Badmouthing competition is like a cancer in our politically correct culture. Does competition make life more difficult? You bet it does, but that's one way we make things better! We grow and mature through adversity. Our skills improve when they are tested, and that's to our benefit, not our detriment.

And low self-esteem? Give me a break. Here's the only self-esteem you need, and it's the one thing you don't have to earn: You are a valuable human being by the grace of being alive. Because of who you are, you matter to yourself, your family, your friends, your higher power—to whomever or whatever is important in your life. The Declaration of Independence acknowledges that we are born "with certain inalienable rights . . . Life, Liberty and the pursuit of Happiness." That's everything you need to get anything you want. You're not *entitled* to anything else. Notice there's not anything in there about an "inalienable right" to a jet ski or an iPod or a house in the Hollywood Hills.

Your will and your self are your birthrights. Everything else is up to you.

The only way to improve your self-image is to improve yourself, and that comes through achievement. And, as you now know, we achieve through competition—overcoming some obstacle or doing something better or faster or more effectively than other people. The results of our own hard work lead to better goods and services for everybody—a safer, more efficient, and more opportunity-filled world and a higher quality of life. From this small truth flows nothing less than progress itself.

One more thing. Many people criticize American free markets and free enterprise because they depend on competition, creating winners and losers. But no one who's trying remains a loser forever. The experience of losing is like being handed a set of instructions for doing things better next time. You get to see first-hand what works and what doesn't. And there's always room for additional winners at the top.

In the old Soviet Union the economy was planned from the top down, and the state owned all the resources. A few self-appointed government experts decided everything, asserting that they could anticipate every need and address every problem better than entrepreneurial individuals. The results? People ended up standing in line for bread, among other things. If you're too young to remember, you can look it up.

In Cuba, where the economy is planned by a cadre of government officials, the average monthly salary is

$19 (a brain surgeon makes $22,[1] in case you're wondering what the top end is).

In North Korea, where the most brutal communist regime in history still reigns supreme, between 600,000 and 2.5 million people starved to death in the 1990s.[2] Think about that: People died for lack of food in a world where, by contrast, citizens of capitalistic countries don't experience food shortages or starvation.

I could go on and on with this list, but the point I want you to know is this: Free enterprise is your friend. It can be tough, but there's always opportunity to better yourself, and that's what makes it so attractive and so useful. Other systems simply don't allow that. Competition drives quality. Competition is the engine of hope. Competition is the pathway to improvement and opportunity, and that's why I'm insanely committed to competition.

Look at the competitors I leave in the dust every day. Are they hurting? Not really. They're not doing nearly as well as I am, but that's to their benefit: It

---

1. "Cuban Salaries Rise to $19 a Month," *Ahram Online*, June 5, 2012, http://english
.ahram.org.eg/News/43876.aspx.
2. Joshua Stanton and Sung-Yoon Lee, "Pyongyang's Hunger Games," *New York Times*, March 7, 2014, http://www.nytimes.com/2014/03/08/opinion/pyongyangs
-hunger-games.html?_r=1.

encourages them to perfect what they do. Besides, all this hard work to get better reaches far beyond self-improvement. Who else benefits?

The people who depend on me, that's who. Competition drives me to hone my skills at improving the outcome for my clients.

Sadly, they no longer teach any of this truth in school. Too controversial, they say. *Too divisive. Too damaging to one's precious self-esteem.*

They may not tell you the truth about competition any more, but I just did. The sooner you're aware of its power, the sooner you'll achieve your dream. Whatever skill you have, wherever you want to excel, recognize the power of competition, and use it. Be *insanely committed to competition.*

JZ's CHAPTER TIPS

» Success is driven by competition.

» Recognize the value of competition.

» The only way to improve your self-image is to improve yourself, and that comes through relentless commitment and hard work.

» There's always room for more winners at the top.

» Free enterprise is your friend.

BE INSANELY COMMITTED TO YOUR OWN PROFESSIONALISM.

CHAPTER 6

I'm great at advertising. I've proven that. But being great at what you do is still not quite enough. If you want to make it all the way to your goal, all the way to the top, you have to match your skill with an insane commitment to professionalism.

Professionalism is a word people hear all the time, but it's useless unless you put it into action. Much of the insanity I've told you about so far requires you to turn your attention to yourself, but now we're looking at what we can do for others. So here's what an insane commitment to professionalism entails:

- It means giving your very best to everyone around you.

- It means giving people *more* than they asked for—value on top of value.

- It means competing not just against the other guy but also against a standard of quality that stands the test of time.

- It means self-discipline in all things—not just to show how strong you are but also to improve the experience for someone else.

The men and women who do business in this way set an example for the rest of us, and they are rare. You need to be one of them.

It's not easy to do, though. Human beings aren't born with a natural inclination to perform their best in the face of even the slightest adversity. Our instinct is to just get it done and go on. We think that "good enough" is good enough.

This tendency worms its way into the smallest things. When you wake up in the morning, your first thought is probably to hit that snooze bar and, a few minutes later, to hit it again. For many of you, the only reason you don't keep banging that button is that you know your boss will kick your ass if you show up late.

When my alarm goes off in the morning—well, the truth is, my alarm doesn't go off. I wake up before that happens. My alarm isn't my signal to start the day; it's my insurance policy in case I somehow sleep past 4 a.m. (That hasn't happened yet, but I like to cover my bases.) I get up and get started, and I don't loll around drinking coffee and watching morning chat shows. I get dressed and begin being productive.

This may come as a shock to you, but that behavior does not come naturally—not to me or anybody else. I'm not some freak of nature who gets moving in the morning because my DNA tells me to. But over the years I have disciplined myself to ignore my natural inclination to do the easy thing. Instead, I choose to be productive.

You can do it too. You simply make the correct choice over and over again! That's easy to say but hard to do. Why? Because it takes strength of will, it takes character, and it takes an insane commitment to professionalism.

When you encounter a situation where there's a

choice, ask yourself, *What's the best choice?* Do not ask yourself, *What's the easy choice?* Easy or hard doesn't enter into it. If you want to be a person of character, you do the right thing, regardless.

After all, you are in pursuit of a dream, and you will not achieve professionalism without strong character and sound decisions.

After a few weeks, a few months, or however long it takes, making this choice is going to get easier. I know that's true because that's been the case for all successful people, including me. When I made up my mind to achieve my dream, one of the first things I decided was to make the right and wise choice in every situation, regardless of how difficult it might be. I wanted my dream more than I wanted the easy life.

I started practicing that attitude when I was a kid getting up in the middle of the night for my paper route. I kept it up when I hired other kids to work on that route, which took a lot more willpower than it would have taken to just sneak out and do the early-morning run against my mother's orders.

I was lucky to face that challenge then, because it gave me an early start on building a commitment to professionalism.

It may be too late for you to start early, but it's not too late to start for the rest of your life.

By the way, if you're waiting for me to give you a shortcut, keep waiting. It's not going to happen. Like every good thing in life, professionalism depends on you, your will, and your own hard work. It's a matter of your character and your commitment.

Did you ever see the movie *Pulp Fiction*? Near the end, there's a short scene that underscores this point. The great actor Harvey Keitel plays Winston Wolfe, a man who can get you out of any jam. Mr. Wolfe says, "Just because you are a character doesn't mean that you have character." That's a pretty smart line, even if it does come from a cinematic gangster.

I'm sure you know people who get away with murder because they're funny or handsome or beautiful or smart. Those kinds of people are everywhere, including the world of business. They think they can act like divas because the quality of their work is so good. Believe me, that attitude never works for long. Character counts. I'll take a modestly talented guy with self-discipline and real commitment any day over a so-called genius who's difficult to work with. If you're unreliable and unpredictable, I don't have time for you, no matter what you can do. Professionals want to be around other professionals.

The comedian Tina Fey wrote the same thing in her book, *Bossypants* (New York: Reagan Arthur/Little, Brown, 2013). When she was the head writer for *Saturday Night Live* and the show *30 Rock*, she said she'd always hire *reliable* people for her staff over the crazy comedy writers who wrote fantastic material but otherwise picked fights and showed up only when the mood struck. I'm with her: Give me smart and reliable. Give me men and women of character. Professionals. Genius only goes so far.

After all, behind every prima donna genius is another genius coming up fast, one minus the arrogance. Competition to the rescue! There's bound to be someone else out there as good as the diva but without the baggage of unprofessionalism and unreliability.

Building your reputation is a never-ending job. Every time they see you, the people who rely on you (or who might decide to rely on you later) are reassessing you as an employee, a partner, a client, a supplier, a boss, a vendor, or whatever it is you do. When it comes to being a reliable professional, you can't take a day off. You can't even take an hour off!

With every choice that affects your behavior, you're either impressing someone or you're making that person think less of you. When it comes to human interaction, there is no neutral position: To *do nothing* to promote your reputation is to *diminish* that reputation. In fact, your greatest asset is your reputation.

Success demands insane commitment to being a professional. Do you have it?

When you say you'll do something, do you do it every time?

When it comes time to deliver, do you produce what you promised, or do you make excuses for your shortcomings?

Are you the individual who strives to exceed expectations?

Do you treat everyone the way you yourself would like to be treated?

Will you move heaven and earth to keep your promises?

If you want to have the success in life that drove you to read this book in the first place, be insanely committed to professionalism.

JZ's CHAPTER TIPS

» Resist the urge to do the easy thing. Instead, do the right thing. Make the right choice.

» Genius only goes so far.

» Build and maintain your reputation; it is your greatest asset.

BE INSANELY COMMITTED TO THE PEOPLE WHO RELY ON YOU.

CHAPTER 7

Success demands insane commitment to many things: improving your skills, using competition to get better, delivering the best quality products and services, and sacrificing whatever it takes to achieve what you want out of life.

That's a pretty thorough list, but it's still one point short. Turns out my insanity runs pretty deep!

I'm also insanely committed to the people who rely on me.

I used to hear this as a kid: "If you say you're going to do something, then stand up and do it." I had told my mom I wouldn't sneak out, and I had an agreement with the paper to deliver copies every morning. I wasn't about to break either of those promises. I searched until I found a way to do what I said I would do! It's all about keeping your word.

The greatest success, though, goes to those of us who can extend that commitment and instill it in others. When I'm insanely committed to people, I make them so accustomed to having the very best that they don't even *think* of working with anyone else. To put it another way, I am really creating, in them, an insane commitment to me, my work, and my company.

Think of anyone in your life who depends on what you produce. Your job must be to get them addicted to you, and when I say "addicted," that's exactly what I mean.

Get them hooked. Give them something they cannot get along without. Give it to them in every interaction. And make sure it's something that is vital to their own efforts to reach their goals. (When it comes to their success, always assume they are as passionate as you are. Use this to your advantage.)

When somebody gets hooked on something, he or she is no longer able to function without it, so the people you work with need to become dependent on what you do. Your work needs to be of such high quality and so vital to them that they cannot imagine how they would get along without it.

Imagine being on the receiving end of that kind of insane commitment—to have people going way above and beyond what they have to do, simply because they want you to succeed. To have them do everything they can to support your efforts, even when it's so far from their job description that you start to wonder what's in it for them. Wouldn't you love to have somebody like that in your life? And wouldn't you become insanely loyal to them? Of course you would.

So go be that person for others: your clients, your partners, your boss, and maybe—just maybe—someone who can help you achieve your dream.

Behold, the Jordan Zimmerman "insanity" in action!

You may say, "Well, Jordan, that sounds like a great idea, but you don't know how unimportant my job is. I'm at the very bottom of the operation. Nobody even knows I'm there, and I could be replaced tomorrow."

Oh, really? That's the kind of narrow, hope-stealing, self-defeating thinking that's been holding you back.

What you do is only as unimportant as you let it be. You can blend into the wallpaper like a nobody or you can make yourself useful.

You're only as unimportant as you make yourself. More often than you realize, the big wheels in life started as little gears. Many successful people began as interns and went on to make great careers for themselves. A couple of years ago, Judith Aquino at *Business Insider* researched the career paths of interns. Some are now entrepreneurs who founded their own companies, some are now leaders who drive entire industries, and some have changed the world:[3]

- Steven Spielberg started out as an intern at Universal Studios and then became the youngest director the company ever signed to a long-term deal.

- In 2011 Ursula Burns became the first female African-American chairman and CEO of Xerox, a company she joined as an intern in 1980.

- Andrew Ross Sorkin is a renowned business journalist and a columnist for the *New York Times*,

---

3. Judith Aquino, "12 Successful People Who Started as Interns," *Business Insider*, June 2, 2011, http://www.businessinsider.com/12-famous-people-who-paid-their-dues-as-interns-2011-6?op=1.

where he began as an intern when he was a senior in high school.

- Betsey Johnson is the queen of unusual and wildly popular fashions for women. Before she was the head of her own fashion label, she was an intern at *Mademoiselle* magazine.

- Did you ever see the movie *The Pursuit of Happyness*? That's the story of Chris Gardner, a man who was homeless and living on the street. An internship would have been a step up for him, and that's exactly what he realized, so he worked his ass off to get one. He set his sights on more than just any internship. He earned a prestigious and hard-to-get internship at Dean Witter Reynolds and then went on to become the head of his own brokerage firm.

- Even the great Steve Jobs, a man I admire greatly, began as an intern at Hewlett-Packard.

Every one of those people moved ahead because, from the very beginning, they understood that no job is too small and no task is too insignificant not to be useful in a multitude of ways—useful to the person doing it and useful to the person or organization being served. You can learn something about an industry or a career or a business, and you can also use that as a way to show the people in charge—those who can help you reach your goal—that you are valuable, industrious, and even indispensible.

Insane commitment to the people who depend on you can yield spectacular progress, but how *much* progress depends entirely on you. If you take whatever you have to do and make it into something indispensible, you will have distinguished yourself and set yourself above roughly 99 percent of everybody else out there.

While the rest of the world whines with their my-dog-ate-my-homework excuses for whatever it is they didn't get done, your attitude will be *whatever it takes*. You keep your word in everything, big or small. You find ways to contribute that are above and beyond your responsibilities. And when everybody else is turning off the lights and going home, you're looking for yet another way to do more. You are insanely committed to exceeding expectations.

And when you're insanely committed to the people who rely on you, obstacles become opportunities. As

Winston Churchill supposedly said, "If you're going through hell, keep going."

The perseverance that you demonstrate and the commitment that you make are what make you indispensible—and another good kind of insane.

JZ's CHAPTER TIPS

» Do what you say you are going to do. Keep your word.

» Don't be a wallflower. Differentiate yourself and showcase your value.

» Be insanely committed to exceeding expectations.

» Do whatever it takes.

» As Winston Churchill said, if you're going through hell, keep going.

PART II

PRIDE, EXCUSES, AND LIES YOU TELL YOURSELF

NO EXCUSES.

CHAPTER 8

There are no excuses in life.

I've been running a business since I was nine years old, and I've dealt with thousands of employees, so believe me, I've heard every excuse there is:

I don't have the tools I need.

I don't have the right report.

I let myself get too busy with something else.

The people I work with screwed it up.

Somebody didn't give me all the data I need.

I didn't know you wanted this today.

I didn't know you wanted this at all.

On and on it goes, the pathetic litany of excuses,

every one an admission of failure, every one unaccept-able. There's only one thing anyone can say in this situation that earns even the tiniest bit of respect from me: *No excuse, sir. It's my own damned fault.*

That's the only excuse that even sort of works for me, and it only works once. Give me excuses a sec-ond time, and that'll be the last time, because then I'll know you're just not trying hard enough and not working smart enough. Do what you say you'll do, or go work for somebody else. You can't work for my company and make excuses. My company and my life are built on *no excuses.*

Think about it: Every excuse comes down to assign-ing blame to other people when, in pretty much every situation, more diligence on your part would have made things come out right. Whether you pin your failure on some other guy in the office, the client, the tools, or somebody else not around to defend himself, it's all the same.

Stop passing the buck, okay? That's not hard to learn.

And if you start paying attention to the excuses you hear every day, you'll quickly notice a pattern: You rarely hear excuses about work that's fun or easy.

People act like they'll move heaven and earth to get that stuff done, because they know they'll never actually have to move heaven and earth. Everybody likes doing fun stuff! But when it comes to the hard stuff, one obstacle and they're out to lunch.

Instead, be the person who keeps your goal in mind. Be the person who does the work that you committed to do—and don't take the easy way out. Embrace challenging work, and recognize that it is an opportunity.

And if you are that rare person who keeps a promise or meets an obligation instead of begging off, congratulations. You're already on the road to success: You're telling yourself *no excuses*.

For everybody else—priorities! It's all about priorities. When faced with a choice, many people will do what matters to them at the expense of their promises. They think that a choice like that has few consequences—that they can get away with it—but they're wrong. Don't lie to me, and don't lie to yourself.

Settling for excuses when the hard choices come along just pushes your destination further into the future. Push it out far enough, and you'll lose sight of it completely, and you'll never get there at all.

If you're going to be successful, remember: *no excuses.*

The worst kind of excuse is blaming your personal life for your professional shortcomings. As an employer, I have no patience for somebody I depend on giving me a sorry line about fighting with his wife, wrangling with her husband, arguing with a girlfriend or a boyfriend, or getting in some disagreement with mom or dad or a son or a daughter. What matters to me is work. When you work for me, you *work* for me. Leave home at home.

I'm sure you are familiar with abbreviations for text messages such as SMH (shaking my head), RTM (read the manual), LOL (laugh out loud), and others. Here's one from Jordan Zimmerman. Feel free to use it anytime: IDFC. It stands for *I don't effing care.* I should get an ink stamp on my desk, and when someone walks in with an excuse, I'll grab that guy by the collar and stamp it on his forehead.

You say you had a bad night last night? IDFC.

You say your wife is mad at you? IDFC.

You say your kid wouldn't do his homework so you stayed up half the night dealing with it? IDFC.

You may think I'm heartless. Think what you like. IDFC. Part of achieving your dreams is learning to keep private things private. I wrote this book to help you find your way to success, not to wipe your nose and tell you everything's going to be all right.

Guess what? If you don't take charge of your life, it's not going to be all right. Things don't work themselves out. You have to do that yourself. I'm here to help you learn a few things about the road to success: First, recognize that successful people are infinitely reliable. They do not make excuses. The people who depend on you don't hire you so they can be your friends. They hire you to get things done faster and better than anybody else, *as you promised you would.* That's what they're paying you for, remember?

You've been reading my book. Have you seen one word of complaint about my personal life? Of course not. If I had an argument with my wife, you'd never know. I don't bring my problems into the office, and there's none of that in these pages. You're reading this book because you want me to tell you how to get off your ass and be successful.

I tell you about my hard times not to get your sympathy—IDFC. I tell you about my hard times so you can learn from them and put that knowledge to use.

One more thing: Blaming failure on your personal

life has more consequences than simply demonstrating weakness. Don't spend mental energy on personal problems when you're supposed to be spending it on professional goals. That will leave you working at less than full capacity, with less than total creativity, and well below your best on every front. Trying to work while you brood on problems at home is like trying to hit a baseball with one eye covered. Sure, you might still hit it, but you won't hit it as often, you won't hit it as hard, and it won't go as far. Separate the personal from the professional. Whether you're working for yourself or someone else, give it all you have. Don't you dare waste their time on your problems.

Personal-life excuses are the sorriest excuses there are. You're appealing to nothing but pity, and that won't buy you a pass, at least not at any first-tier operation, which is where you want to be. I don't have time for that kind of nonsense and neither does any other successful person. Make a friend, buy a dog, find someone to tell your troubles to. But don't make excuses to the people who rely on you.

Do your job, and deal with your personal problems on your own effing time.

IDFC.

JZ's CHAPTER TIPS

» No excuses. Excuses are admissions of failure.

» Successful individuals keep their word, follow through, and are infinitely reliable.

» There is no room for your personal life in your business life. Don't bring it to work. Leave it at home.

» IDFC.

QUIT BEING PROUD. NO JOB IS BENEATH YOU.

CHAPTER 9

The road to success is often blocked by obstacles that exist only in your mind. Lack of money, for instance. That's no obstacle. You can always come up with a little more, and you can always get along with a little less. A lack of big ideas. Sorry. Every creative, ambitious, committed person I know wakes up in the morning with another good idea. Somebody somewhere is keeping you down? Hey, that's the story of mankind. Everyone has to do battle with the world. You don't have it tougher than anybody else right now or anybody else ever.

So let me ask you this: If you're as great as you think you are—filled with potential and imagination and ideas—and you're destined for all this success, how come you're not there yet?

Really. *Why are you still so far from where you want to be?* Your problem may be ego and pride. Your biggest obstacle could be you.

If you want to succeed, move beyond vanity. Get down in the dirt. Immerse yourself in the messy, demanding work of becoming a success. And remember: No job is beneath you. In fact, it's the only way up. I speak from experience.

Have you ever heard somebody in a start-up say that he's the "chief cook and bottle washer"? That means he does everything. He may be the captain of the ship, but he's not afraid to get his hands dirty and swab the deck. He will do any and every job that comes along.

When I started my advertising business, that was me: I did *everything*, and I mean I did literally everything. I didn't just do what a boss is supposed to do. I was sweeping the floors because when you're just beginning, you have to be ready, willing, and able to do anything that needs to be done. I wanted success, and I was willing to do anything to get it.

That has to be your attitude. Pride has no place in your life.

If you refuse to let go of your pride, let me tell you who you're going to be, or maybe who you already are: You're a legend but only in your own mind. You're that clown at the party who's always talking about his next big plan but who never has anything to show for the last one.

If you're that guy or gal, you may not know it, but it's obvious to the people around you. Everybody has your number.

You don't want to end up being that guy. I know that. That's why you're reading this book. But you have to let go of that arrogance, air of superiority, and ego.

Pride is simply a roadblock to winning. If you give up your pride and do every job that comes along, no matter how menial it might seem, you will learn how any business really and truly works. If you're going to be a leader, that's an indispensible truth to have in your head.

When I started Zimmerman Advertising, I found the clients, landed the deals, came up with the advertising plans, wrote the copy, and did the proofreading. I worked with the art director to get the look of a job just perfect. I even made sure the spacing in the text was right! Then I spent time with the clients to be sure they were satisfied, and I made it my responsibility to hand deliver the ads to the newspapers.

I was tearing down my pride, sure, but I was doing what had to be done, and I was also learning how the business works. There was no job beneath me—none, not ever.

Whatever opportunity you want to pursue, there are multiple levels of operation and expertise that support it, filled with hundreds of jobs and thousands of responsibilities. You should know something about all of them.

Here's one more reason to learn all those jobs: If you know firsthand what people are supposed to be doing, they can never pull the wool over your eyes. There's a lot that goes on today at Zimmerman, but I'm a successful leader today in part because I can walk into any office in any of our locations and (1) understand what's going on, and (2) know how to get to the bottom of something that has gone wrong.

That doesn't mean I can do any given job better than the great people I've hired. I hired them because they're the best at what they do. I want them to impress me. I want them to exceed my expectations. I want them to be better than I am at that job. I demand it! And you know what? They have no excuse for not being better than me. They're focusing their tremendous skills full time on making one particular job the very best it can be. That's the way you get a solid final product.

In order to lead, I don't have to master every skill; I just need to understand them. I'd be wasting my energy trying to be proficient at everything, and there isn't enough time, anyway. If you want to prepare a delicious meal, you don't have to slaughter the cow and raise the vegetables, but you damn well better know how to recognize the finest cuts of meat and the best produce. It's the same in building a business.

In working toward your goal, your job is to understand what's going on at each and every step as you climb up that ladder. There is deep value in that kind of deep understanding. Knowing things from the ground up—*really* knowing things—comes only from firsthand experience. And if I had said, "I'm the leader. I can't be bothered with that," I would not have become the success I am today.

Nothing is beneath you. Do the job. Learn. It'll make you a better coach for everybody in the end.

Start by putting away your pride.

JZ's CHAPTER TIPS

» The road to success is full of obstacles.

» Put aside your ego and your pride.

» No job is beneath you.

» Knowing and understanding the operation inside and out ensures you will be able to identify what's going right and what's going wrong.

» There is no substitute for firsthand experience. It yields deep knowledge.

LIFE IS UNFAIR. SUCCEED ANYWAY.

CHAPTER 10

There's nothing inherently noble, helpful, or hurtful about coming from humble beginnings. Life is exactly what you make of it—nothing less and not a damn thing more.

I come from humble beginnings. I grew up in a little town in New Jersey called Old Bridge—exit 12 off the New Jersey Turnpike (that's how you give directions in Jersey), about 45 minutes from New York City.

Big deal. There's nothing impressive about that and certainly nothing advantageous.

But there is something of value in everything, if you decide to look for it. Here's something I learned from growing up in Old Bridge.

As a kid, it seemed like whenever I heard grown-ups talking, they were arguing with each other and bitching about their lives—not my mom and dad, thank goodness, but everybody around them. That bellyaching was always about the same two things: (1) how much they worried about having enough money to pay their bills at the end of the month and (2) how much they hated their jobs, which they had to go to, to pay those damn bills.

They say a kid's brain is like a sponge, it soaks up whatever's around it. Maybe that's why so many kids grow up to be unhappy adults because all they heard was complaining. But for whatever reason—probably good parenting (as you'll read in a minute) or maybe just the early onset of that Jordan Zimmerman insanity—I had a different reaction entirely. I rejected all that whining instinctively! I could not imagine being headed for the miserable existence of most of the adults I knew. I made up my mind early on that I wasn't going to allow that to happen. I figured life could not possibly be as bad as it seemed everybody in Old Bridge thought it was.

But I didn't know for sure. How could I? I was a kid! So I asked the only expert I knew, my dad.

When I was eight years old, I sat down with my dad

for a serious talk, boy to man. I said, "Dad, I hear all these adults complaining about how hard it is to be a grown-up. They don't like their jobs. They don't have enough money. That's not the way it really is, is it?"

And with his answer, my father, God bless him, set me on the road not only to success but also to a truly satisfying life. Here's what he said, as I remember it decades later, as I've replayed it with him over dinner recently, and as I've lived it every day:

"Jordan," he told me, "they're not unhappy because they want to be. They're unhappy because they took whatever life handed them instead of making their own way."

As usual, Dad had my attention. This was a big idea for a kid to hear, and I was all ears.

"Some of them didn't focus in grade school and high school. Some of them didn't go on to get a good education beyond that. That lack of learning? That's a huge mistake, son, because education is something you can't do without! But the biggest mistake of all that they made was this: They didn't find a career they were passionate about.

"With no goal and no passion to guide their decisions, life just happened to them. They did what was

right in front of them, what they saw other people
doing that was simple to get, quick to finish, and
didn't take any planning. Son, they took instant gratification. If you don't know the value of discipline and
patience and hard work, you're going to fall for instant
gratification every single time."

I asked my dad what that meant, instant gratification.

"It means settling for what's easy. You see how their
lives have played out. But you hear it, too, and that's
where those conversations came from. They married
at a young age. They had kids at a young age. They
took whatever jobs they could find to pay the bills.
And then they were stuck—stuck having to pay those
bills, stuck having to meet obligations, stuck in a life
that they fell into instead of planned. All that heartache
and discontent came because it's easier to be the one
life happens to instead of the one who makes a life."

When you're eight years old, that's a lot to take in.
But I understood. So I asked what to me was the obvious question, "How do you avoid that?"

Dad didn't miss a beat: "It takes real discipline to
look ahead, make a plan, prepare yourself for it, and
stick to it. That's especially true when you're young,

and you think you have all the time in the world. But that doesn't excuse not doing it, son. You have to say, 'I am going to pick a target and drive relentlessly for that target and get the things I want. First and foremost, I am going to educate myself. That way I am going to be equipped to make the life I want, and then I will be truly prepared later to take on those obligations— marriage, a family—that can be so fulfilling. Those obligations will then be an enriching part of my life, as they ought to be, instead of becoming something that makes me resentful and hangs over my every decision.'"

I said, "Dad, I think I get it, but where do I start?"

"Simple," Dad said. "Find your passion."

Bingo. And what my dad said to me years ago is what I say to you now: Find something that excites you so much that you want to do it every day. Don't ask how much money it will earn you or how hard it might be to achieve or how far away it seems right now. Then start running toward that goal.

You will not always be the smartest, but you can always be the one who works the hardest, and that will almost always make up for lack of knowledge. Whatever you do, you have to have a never-quit attitude. You have to understand that when you wake up every morning, you're blessed to be here, blessed to be breathing, walking, talking, living, and learning. Appreciate every day you have by making use of it.

If you do what I'm telling you, you'll get what you want, and best of all, you will have yourself to thank for it, courtesy of your commitment, positive attitude, and hard work.

JZ's CHAPTER TIPS

» Unhappy people do not choose to be unhappy. They are unhappy, because they accepted what life handed them.

» Make your life. Don't let life just happen to you.

» Find your passion.

ATTACK OF THE
BULLSHITTERS!

CHAPTER 11

The world is full of professional bullshitters. You
know the kind: fancy suits, big microphones, strut-
ting around in front of a huge audience of mindless,
nodding simpletons. All they're selling—and believe
me, they're *selling it*—is a shoeshine and a smile.

Bunch of useless happy talk, that's all it is.

I don't want to name names. (Actually, I *do* want
to name names. I want to rattle off a whole bunch of
them! But my attorney says it's smarter to let you, the
reader, imagine who I might be talking about, instead
of putting those names in print. Anyway, *you* know
exactly who I'm talking about. Just turn on the TV.)

The bullshitters have a pretty free rein on TV and across the Internet. Once in a great while, though, you meet someone who stands out from that pack, somebody who offers you real value. What's the difference? That person brings experience, real-world experience in building something other than her very own happy-talk empire. If you're going to listen to someone, you want a person who, through her own sweat and hard work, has created something that provides a product or a service that people really need:

Something that makes life easier or more enjoyable.

Something that makes doing business a little more practical.

Something that helps.

Something of quality.

Something of *value* beyond self-serving claims.

Most of the people you meet who have that kind of experience aren't standing in front of auditorium crowds, preening in front of a video wall, and selling their junk in the lobby like T-shirt vendors at a rock concert. The vast majority of the good guys—men and women with both the heartfelt desire to help you get ahead and the experience to equip you for the journey—are busy working on their own dreams and visions on a daily basis.

When you find one of these people, latch on to him or her, and really listen to what he or she says. Watch carefully. Follow closely. Learn.

Like I said, my buddy the lawyer said I shouldn't name names, but he didn't say I couldn't use a name I made up! There's one particular "you can do it!" guy out there who really bugs the hell out of me. Let's call him Timmy Tomorrow. He's the king of self-help. He's on TV all the time in nauseating half-hour infomercials, selling the same advice books, CDs, and DVDs over and over again but slapping different titles on them.

Next time you see Timmy Tomorrow on television, stop for a few minutes. Think about what he's saying. Then apply The Test. It's an easy way to tell the difference between the bullshitters and the men and women of character, vision, and achievement who are the real deal. Ask yourself: *What has Timmy Tomorrow actually done? Did he build a business in the real world? Did he deal with competition and failure and hardship? Did he figure out a way around the obstacles that presented themselves on his unique road to success? And is he offering you what he learned along the way so you could do it for yourself?*

Or is he just creating hype?

Let him talk. Listen for details. Listen for experience: *Is he giving you practical advice based on his own hard-won achievement, or is he giving you a pep talk?*

The answer is going to be obvious. The Timmy Tomorrow I have in mind sells pep talks. He gives you a hype transplant, and let me tell you something, hype doesn't last. Actually, Timmy sells a lot more than words. He has a whole warehouse full of DVDs and CDs! Write Timmy a check, and you can take him along wherever you go.

What Timmy is selling is Timmy. I say, keep your wallet in your pocket.

The only thing Timmy gets right is the goal: He wants you to succeed—of course he does. It's good for his business! I agree with the goal too. I want people to succeed. I want you to succeed. But as I've been saying, and as you've probably figured out by now, you learn the most from someone who has done it himself, who has built a business or a career and created his own success.

People who have done that have my respect. They succeed because they have programmed themselves for greatness and surrounded themselves with the right people to make it happen again and again. That's definitely not Timmy Tomorrow or his merry band of hero-worshipers, hangers-on, and sycophants.

Chances are that the mentors and advisors who *will* help you don't spend any time in front of an audience, handing out smiles and "attaboys" and little else. The men and women you need to learn from are up early every day building the next success, climbing the next mountain, for themselves and their families and the people who depend on them.

Learn to recognize the bullshitters, and don't waste your precious time or money on their useless advice. Instead, seek lessons from those who have built real businesses and real lives from the ground up.

JZ's CHAPTER TIPS

» Hype doesn't last.

» You will learn the most from the individual who has the hard work and accomplishments to back up his or her knowledge.

» Successful people program themselves for greatness and then surround themselves with the right people to sustain that greatness.

» The men and women you need to learn from are rarely on a stage. They're busy building the next success.

YOU CAN'T BUILD A
BETTER HORSE.

CHAPTER 12

There are two kinds of change in the world. Only two. There's the kind that happens a little at a time so you don't really notice. Then there's the kind that grabs you by the collar and turns your whole world upside down.

That first kind is the kind we know best. It's what we sometimes think of as "progress," even though that's not quite what it is. I'm talking about the little improvements that come along every few months or years in a slow process that you don't see. Think of how the software on your computer gets updated. Maybe it becomes a little easier to use, maybe the speed picks up, but it happens in such small increments over such a long period of time that you barely notice. Compare the laptop you have today with the one you had six or seven years ago. Does this new one run a little faster, a little smoother? Probably. But it's hard to tell, because the overall experience is pretty much the same today as it was a few years back.

Change like that has its place—call it maintenance—but it doesn't make us rethink everything we've been doing in our life. It's what I call "small change," like those pennies in the dish at the 7-Eleven. More to the point, no matter how many pennies you scrape together, you'll never get rich. And it's the same with this journey you're on to achieve success. No matter how much small change you manage to amass, you'll never transform your life that way. What it takes is deep-rooted, big-deal change—a true transformation.

Now think about the other kind of change— tear-the-roof-off-the-dump, put-a-man-on-the-moon, turn-the-world-upside-down change. When that happens, look out!

For centuries people traveled from point A to point B on the back of a horse or in a horse-drawn wagon. Suppose Henry Ford had asked people what they needed most in the realm of transportation, they would have answered, "Build me a faster horse." But there's only so much you can do to improve a horse. You might get a better saddle or better horseshoes, or maybe you could somehow train the horse to run faster. It's a long shot, but you could give it a try. Yet even if you succeeded, all you would have done was shave a few minutes off a long trip.

Well, Henry Ford didn't ask, and no one spoke up. He just listened to his gut and invented the gas-powered automobile.

From where we stand today, slow and inefficient travel in the past looks like a real problem, but the people of that day didn't see it like that. *Sure*, they might have said, *it would be nice to have a faster and more convenient way to travel, but that's not realistic.*

I'll bet you've heard that before about your own life: *Sure, it would be nice to have a better career or your own business or whatever it is you're dreaming about, but that's not realistic.* Sometimes we hear it from other people, but most often what stops us is when we hear it from ourselves.

Keep reading.

When it came to personal transportation, what people needed was a transformative experience, something more than a faster horse. They needed something that leaped past the current way of doing things to something entirely different. The world was waiting for someone who would stop trying to upgrade what existed and instead would start over with the original problem—finding the fastest way to get from point A to point B.

A century ago Henry Ford wanted to transform the whole idea of transportation, and he knew the answer was not going to be incremental improvements—not small change. The solution was going to take imagination, and that's something Ford had plenty of.

Not only that. He matched his imagination with experience and hard-won knowledge to give us the automobile—and with it came a whole new era not only in transportation but also in pretty much everything else in the world. Ford's invention caused ripples out in every direction, creating new industries and revolutionizing old ones and transforming life across the globe.

Would we have an oil industry without the automobile? Not really. Would we have a system of safe and durable roads that lead from any point in the country to any other? No way! Would we have spectacular advances in design and safety and efficiency for the mechanical things we use every day? Maybe not. And there's more, big and small—from creating a new dynamic of global power to the creation of the drive-in.

Henry Ford didn't plan all that because he didn't need to. What he did was embrace his own vision. He didn't go around asking potential customers what they might like. He didn't look at what was out there and then figure out how to make it a little better or a little fancier. He thought of a whole new way to get around. That, in turn, created a new world of opportunity for Ford himself and others.

This type of individual is a true visionary. He is striving for transformational change. He doesn't follow the mindless crowd. He thinks of only this: What revolutionary idea do I have that will solve the problem at hand. How can I best reach my goal?

Small change has its place, but when it comes to transforming your life and reaching your great goal, it has no place at all. Small change is like a new recipe for meatloaf: It may taste a little better, but it's still meatloaf. Surely you can do better than that. We're talking about your life here! When it comes to your goals, your happiness, and your style of life, you deserve more than better meatloaf. Demand it of yourself.

Aim high. Swing for the bleachers.

Great men and women have great vision. What's yours? If it requires only small change, you're not thinking big enough.

Think again. You need transformation.

Go for big change, or don't go!

JZ's CHAPTER TIPS

» Success requires you to make significant change to your life.

» Do not settle for minimal improvement.

» Do not pay attention to the mindless crowd.

» Great men and women have great vision. What's yours? If it requires only small change, you're not thinking big enough.

DOING BRAIN SURGERY
ON YOURSELF.

CHAPTER 13

Now I'm going to show you how to do brain surgery—
on yourself.

Biology wasn't my favorite subject as a kid, but I was
dedicated to learning. I still am. So everything I was
supposed to learn, I threw myself into. For instance,
I learned that there's a special modulatory system in
the brain called the reticular activating system (RAS).
The RAS is the system that controls breathing, sleep-
ing, waking, and heartbeats. What's really interesting
about the RAS is that it allows you to will yourself to
do anything you want to do.

The RAS switches you into and out of paying close attention. What does that mean in daily life? Here's an example: When you go to the airport, you wade through security, you check in, and then you settle into a seat or find a place to stand while you wait to board. But before you turn to something else—checking your email, returning a call, looking through a magazine— you do one other thing. You program your brain to do you a little favor: *If my name or my flight number comes over the loudspeaker, let me hear it. Everything else, I want blocked out.*

You do that unconsciously and automatically, and it works. You know that from your own experience. You can "operate" on your brain with the power of your thoughts, attitudes, and choices. Part of leveraging that power is asserting yourself to yourself. This crazy-sounding idea is effective, because this is how your body works. Your mind is part of your body, so why not tell it to do what you want?

Keeping an ear out for your flight number at the airport is the least of what your RAS can do. In the same way, you can program yourself to accomplish anything you want to do—and now I'm talking about those goals you have for yourself. I have example after example of programming my own mind—enlisting my brain—in service to the things I want to achieve.

As I built my advertising firm, thousands of people told me my results-centered, client-focused idea wouldn't work. I heard no from everybody, and I do mean everybody: ad executives, business leaders, CEOs, college professors, family members, potential competitors, potential clients, total strangers, and friends who thought they were doing me a big favor by telling me I was dreaming too big.

They thought they were saving me heartache. Instead, they were just giving my RAS one more piece of negativity to filter out and keep away from the rest of my brain, which was working hard to get me where I wanted to be.

I didn't listen to naysayers, and you shouldn't, either.

Do you want to play at my level? Do some brain surgery on yourself by telling your RAS to shut out the negative noise. You can program yourself to do anything you want to do.

JZ's CHAPTER TIPS

» You can "operate" on your brain with the power of your own thoughts, attitudes, and choices.

» I don't listen to naysayers, and neither should you.

» Program your brain to shut out the negative noise.

PART III

FAILURE, FEAR, AND FOULING UP

IF YOU WANT SOMEBODY YOU CAN TRUST, TRUST YOURSELF.

CHAPTER 14

The world is full of experts. Some are overrated self-promoters, others have only a few good ideas, and a very few are actually useful. But none of them have the answers to all the challenges in your life. No matter the failure or fear that comes your way, you will always be the best expert about your own life, because no one cares more about your future than you do.

Your unique perspective is the product of your experience, your education, and your gut instinct. Most of the time you are hired to do a job not just for the skills you have but for who you are. That means your way of doing things has value, so treat it that way. If you want others to trust you, trust yourself.

I get paid to make brands successful, because my clients believe I can do that *better* than other agencies. Sometimes, though, people in my position start looking at the money instead of the quality. They become dependent on that cash as if it were a drug, and they stop listening to their instincts and measuring themselves against the best. They start chasing every random thought that falls out of the client's mouth.

Not me. I'd rather get fired doing it my way than continue doing it wrong the client's way.

It's fine to want to please clients, but they're not paying you to take orders. They're paying you to provide something they don't know how to do themselves. They're paying for your expertise. They're investing in your knowledge with the confidence that the investment is going to provide a return.

Don't pursue an inferior strategy just because somebody else thinks it's a great idea, no matter how big a check that person's waving in front of you. I've turned down plenty of business, because I didn't want my company to be reduced to taking notes and following orders. You should turn down that kind of thing too. When you know what's right, do what's right.

At the same time, follow good advice when it comes along, no matter where it comes from. Our company recently completed production of a series of television spots for a big client whose name you'd recognize. I showed them to one of the key members of the client's team, and he said the ads needed to be "more human." I thought about that and realized he was right: The ads would benefit from being warmer and more focused on personal experience. He had a good idea, and I acted on his advice.

But I didn't do it just because it was the client's idea. I did it because it was a smart idea. You may ask yourself, "If that's what the client wants, shouldn't you give it to them regardless?" The answer is an emphatic *no*. Clients are paying for you to exercise your expertise, experience, and professional judgment, not to shake your head up and down and say, "Right, boss," every time they get an idea. They're paying for your wisdom. Give it to them!

No one cares about your future more than you do. Bob Dylan put it best, in a song: "If you want somebody you can trust, trust yourself."

JZ's CHAPTER TIPS

» People who rely on you aren't paying you to take orders. They need you to provide something they cannot do as well.

» Don't follow an inferior strategy, no matter who thinks it's a great idea.

» Do the right thing.

» You will always be the best expert on your own life, because no one cares more about your future than you do.

YOU, TOO, CAN FAIL LIKE ME!

CHAPTER 15

"Failure is not an option." I've written that a lot in this book. But even the most successful people fall short at times. How does that fact of life reconcile with my advice?

Like this: Getting knocked down along the way is to be expected. *The failure is not getting get back up.*

"Failure is not an option" must be your state of mind, because no one else will save you; the choice to get up or to give up is yours and yours alone. If you open the door to self-pity when you encounter hardship along the way to your goal, that only gives you an excuse to give up on your big goal. If you're trying to lose weight and you overeat at lunch, you may say, *Now the whole day is shot. I might as well snack all afternoon and splurge at dinner too.* That one failed meal can lead to one failed day, which will be on your mind the next morning when you tell yourself: *I blew off yesterday, so I might as well blow off today.* If you've ever tried to lose weight, you know what that means: The whole diet is over.

Unless you discipline yourself to have a "no failure" attitude, every setback will lead you to flirt with quitting. *Maybe what I have is not so bad,* you'll say to yourself, forgetting it was your dissatisfaction with that very situation that drove you to your effort. Your goal will never seem more out of reach than when you've suffered the sting of momentary defeat.

Avoid the road to failure by learning what that pathway looks like: First, you will doubt your abilities and discount the confidence that other people have placed in you. Then you will dwell on what you could have done differently. You'll lower your aim, identifying smaller goals, since you didn't hit the target last time. Then you'll start abandoning the vital good habits you were beginning to build, habits such as planning early, preparing thoroughly, and acting with absolute commitment.

If you see those things happening in your life, the solution is simple: Get back to high standards and hard work. I speak from experience: The only way to get through it is to *get through it*. Never allow the cycle of defeat to begin.

Stop dwelling on how you feel and instead take charge of your emotions. Exercise your will. And be encouraged by this fact: Successful people have been right where you are, and they chose to learn from little failures by transforming them into merely temporary setbacks.

In the 1990s my company landed the advertising account for Mitsubishi. After several very good years, they replaced us with another agency. It was not because of anything we had done wrong, it was just that a new CEO wanted to mark his territory. That's business. It happens. But for me, it was the worst kind of failure, the kind I could not have prevented. But that didn't give me license to pity myself or to stop trying to achieve my goals.

By every objective measure we were as effective a firm as we ever were and demonstrably the most effective firm in America. I was determined not to let this setback become a failure.

I hit the road to replace that lost business and refused to surrender to or become a victim of circumstance.

In four short months I returned to my Fort Lauderdale office with $45 million in new contracts. The day I returned, I received a call from Nissan North America, who wanted to hire us *because* we were now freed from our Mitsubishi exclusive! Between that and my travel, we replaced $40 million in lost business with $145 million in new business—a 260 percent increase from where we had been. Nearly two decades later, Nissan is still our client.

That setback wasn't failure at all, but it was up to me to make the decision to get back up. The bad news opened a door to even greater opportunity, and our relentless drive for success let us walk right through it.

It wasn't long ago that Lane Bryant came to us as a client. The company wanted a sexier image, so we put together a sexy TV spot for them. It was so sexy, in fact, that Fox and CBS wouldn't put it on the air!

Failure? Of course not. Failure is not an option.

Where others would see defeat, we saw a new way to help the client! We realized we could reach beyond the typical customers of Lane Bryant, because we had a mini-controversy that would interest everyone in America. There was a sexy ad, of course, but the incident also touched on hot topics like body image and corporate censorship. We asked Americans to raise a stink with the networks until these commercials could be aired. The result? Night after night of mentions on national news and about $40 million worth of media coverage my client didn't have to pay a dime for.

The lesson? Learn to fail like me! We failed right up the ladder of success, and we brought our client with us.

At some point you are going to take a body blow, and it is going to hurt. As Mike Tyson once put it, "Everybody has a plan until he gets punched in the mouth." It doesn't matter whether or not the hit you took was fair. No one promised that it would be. What matters is that you get up off the floor. The word to write down in big letters and look at every day is "persevere."

"Success is not final; failure is not fatal. It is the courage to continue that counts." Churchill said that, and the world was depending on him. Treat every setback as temporary. Persevere. Never give up on the relentless pursuit of your goal.

JZ's CHAPTER TIPS

» Getting knocked down is to be expected.
  Not getting back up is failure.

» Count on no one to save you but you.

» Get up or give up. It's your choice.

» Relentlessly pursue your goal.

FEAR IS FUEL.

CHAPTER 16

Fear is a part of life, but don't let it stop you from doing what you need to do. Fear is fuel! Learn to use it to persevere.

Your mind has only two reactions when it encounters fear. Number one is to stand up for the battle. Number two is to run away. The two choices could not be more different—fight or flight. There's nothing in between. You either stay on the path or you don't, and that choice decisively separates the winners from everybody else.

From now on, when you come up against fear, your first reaction must be to fight on. I don't care how you have reacted to fear before this. What matters is how you're going to react to fear from today on. I say embrace fear and use it. Make it your servant! Stop using fear as an excuse to give up on your goal. Instead turn it into a tool to get you there faster and to make you a stronger, smarter person.

Think about the times you've felt fear—from the smallest hesitation to the biggest decisions of your life. There are always the same miserable feelings: that twist in the pit of your stomach, the doubts about your abilities, the questions about your strength, and the temptation to throw in the towel. All you want is for those sensations to be over.

Now think about those times that you overcame fear. Remember how that felt? Whatever you accomplished really did seem sweeter. The view from the mountaintop was even greater than you imagined. The reason for all that satisfaction? You did more than reach the goal. You reached the goal after beating back the big, scary things in your way. If you think about that for even a minute, it makes perfect sense. What's more satisfying, winning because you beat a tough opponent or winning because the other team didn't show up? Victory is more gratifying when it is earned, and friend, that's the story of every victory in life.

Here's another benefit to overcoming fear. When you win, you learn something important about the fear you just faced and whatever fearsome thing may be in your future. Whether it's a big test, jumping off the high dive, entering a new school, or having an important conversation with your boss—after it's over, you probably tell yourself that you were more worried than you should have been.

So how do you beat fear? It starts with a decision only you can make. Stop listening to all the discouragement that your mind throws at you. Reject that!

And make that decision right now. Choose to reject the negatives that come into your mind. Don't give them a fair hearing. Dismiss them. Move to the next thing.

This new way of thinking will be easier when you make it a habit. Beating your fears whenever they come along is like lifting weights every day: It makes you stronger. It makes you better able to do the job. And just as lifting heavy weights becomes easier and more natural to people who lift every day, overcoming things that scare you can become easier and more natural too. Those little daily efforts to overcome adversity become so much a part of you that eventually you can't imagine any obstacle could be too great. You'll be able to shatter whatever "ceiling" you imagine is holding you down.

How does that work? Simple. While there really is a limit to how much weight a human being can lift, there is no limit on your ability to overcome the fearsome obstacles between you and your goal. The more you do it, the better you get at it. There is no stopping point, as long as you commit yourself to fighting your fears every single time—and then getting up and fighting again on those occasions when you fail.

I'm sure that you overcame fear more than once long before today, and I'll bet I know how you did it: You told yourself that you didn't have a choice. Once you walked to the end of the diving board, you *had* to jump off. Once you found out that the boss could see you right then and only right then, you *had* to go in and have that conversation.

You psyched yourself into believing that there was no other way through the problem. In reality, you could have backed off the diving board and listened to the laughter from the sidelines. You could have canceled that meeting and gone on enduring whatever miserable situation you intended to fix. Instead, you told yourself that there was only one way out, and that was to plow through your fear.

That's the answer now too. Stop thinking of every obstacle as a moment for fight or flight. Think of it as a fight, period. Fear is an obstacle to be overcome, not an opportunity to quit the game.

To the successful, fear creates more desire for victory.

To the successful, fear creates more hunger to reach the goal.

To the successful, fear is inspiration.

Fear is fuel!

How's that been working for me? Glad you asked. When I was starting Zimmerman Advertising, one of the first fears I had to face was the fear of going out on my own. This is as basic it gets, whether you're someone just out of college who wants to move away from home or an entrepreneur contemplating a start-up. I overcame this fear but not at first. For a while—too long—I allowed that fear to keep me from making the leap.

Then a great thing happened: I realized that if I didn't make the move, nothing was ever going to change. Sure, there was the possibility that I might fail, but that was only a possibility. By giving into fear, I had already transformed the *possibility* of failure into the *certainty* of failure. You can't win if you don't get in the game, and I had benched myself before the game began! So I took that first leap beyond fear. Of course, that was hardly the last time I did it.

I learned very quickly that fear is always with you, even after you've reached your goal and moved on to building bigger and better things. Here's an example: Back in 2008, the economy was in decline. The people of our country were experiencing losses in capital, wealth, and income. Sadly, the economy is not much better today. I could reel off an economic analysis of what factors triggered these bad times and why they remain, but instead I will focus on a cause that rarely gets discussed. The problems have lingered because the vast majority of people react to hard times by listening only to their fears. Economic prudence is one thing, but cowardice is something else. Many businessmen and businesswomen, many entrepreneurs, and even many potentially valuable employees have decided that pessimism is more comforting than the hard work of optimism or the harder work of looking for opportunity in an economy where it is increasingly difficult to find.

Back in 2008, as the troubles took hold, I said to my team, "I heard there's a recession—maybe even a slight depression. I choose not to participate. Are you with me?" Before we came up with a specific course of action to navigate the difficult economy, I chose to reject fear outright.

I decided instead to use fear as fuel for inspiration for greater success. While everybody else cut back and waited for someone else to make the first move, I chose to be that someone else.

We doubled down on our efforts, and I ate that fear for breakfast. The pessimists and fearmongers of the business world were wiped out or left barely hanging on. Not us. My company was able to create some of the greatest successes in our history.

Many people—not you, I hope—may think all of that effort sounds like a difficult way to live, especially when I could have coasted through the hard times on my assets and reputation. In fact, I'm asked all the time: "Jordan, why aren't you relaxing on your own private island in the Caribbean somewhere?"

Why? Because that wouldn't be nearly as fulfilling as what I already do every day of the week! I don't want to take victory laps. I don't want to rest in the glory of what I have already achieved.

I never want to stop achieving, which means I need fear—and so do you.

Fear is fuel!

JZ's CHAPTER TIPS

» When you come up against fear, your first reaction must be to fight on.

» Victory is sweeter when you earn it.

» Use fear to persevere.

SCREWING UP AND GETTING SCREWED OVER.

The pursuit of a long-term goal is actually the pursuit of many short-term goals along the way. Once in a while you are going to come up short, and it's going to be your fault. Mistakes are part of the game. What matters is what you do after.

Number 1: Don't beat yourself up over it.

Maybe you fouled up the report, blew the sale, hired the wrong person, or took the wrong job. Maybe you cost your company a lot of money or cost yourself a lot of time.

Let me ask you something: What is the benefit of feeling bad over that? Does it fix the report? No. Does it make the sale? No. Does it get back the lost time or the lost money? Of course not. All it does is waste energy you could be spending on something productive.

One guy who figured that out after a really big mistake is baseball great Pete Rose. Around 1989 he was accused of betting on the sport. He was banned from the game, and two years later Major League Baseball ruled that he could never be inducted into the Hall of Fame in Cooperstown. It was a bitter rebuke, the harshest punishment that could be dispensed to one of the most beloved and successful players ever. Rose denied the accusations, until one day, a decade and a half after the announcement, he realized that he had been wasting the rest of his life over a mistake he couldn't undo. At that point, Rose moved on with his life.

What he did was bad. But even worse is that he spent fifteen years of his life refighting an old and long-decided battle, instead of moving ahead to the next one.

Good for Rose that he finally figured that out. And even though it took him a long time, he finally realized that it's never too late to get back on track after a mistake. When a reporter from the Twin Cities *Pioneer Press* asked him how it felt to be one of the greats of the game, yet forbidden from being considered for the Baseball Hall of Fame, this is what Rose said: "I'm the one who screwed that up. I'm not mad at anybody. If I ever get a second chance, I'll be the happiest guy in the world. But I can't sit here and [gripe] . . . I screwed it up. I just hang in there with a good life, being a good citizen, and hope to get a second chance. And if I don't, there's not a damn thing I can do about it."[4]

Bad things are going to happen to you too. The sooner you can let go, the sooner your life is going to be moving forward again.

Number 2: Learn something from it.

I'm not talking about kindergarten, feel-good stuff: *Do better! Try harder! Remember that you're a winner!* Please. When I say "learn something" from your mistakes, I mean learn something specific.

If you lost a sale because you didn't follow up on

---

4. Bob Sansevere, "Pete Rose Has Gone from Hit King to Sit King," *Twin Cities.com*, *Pioneer Press*, posted April 6, 2013, http://www.twincities.com/ci_22970948/bob -sansevere-pete-rose-has-gone-from-hit.

time, create a specific plan for following up in the future. If you turned in an incomplete report and made your boss mad, go back and identify what you need to create a complete plan and then come up with a schedule for getting those things done in a timely way. Pinpoint the cause of the mistake and ensure you don't do it again. This isn't difficult, but you have to decide to do it.

If you learn from your mistakes, you won't make them as often—perhaps never again. That's the benefit of mistakes. Anything else you invest in your own failure—your valuable time, your thoughts, whatever—just draws energy from other things you should be doing to build your future.

What about the trouble that comes your way through no fault of your own? What's the best way to deal with that? Let me tell you a story.

I hate the fax machine, and it's because of that Mitsubishi experience I told you about. This is the rest of the story, the other lesson I learned.

In 1996 my company, Zimmerman Advertising, was growing like mad. Our primary business was creating advertising for car companies, and we were fantastic at it. We weren't doing just the best work of our lives; we were doing the best work in the industry, period.

We were making money. We were growing. We were enjoying the recognition among our peers. We were the masters of the marketplace. The innovative Mitsubishi Corporation was our biggest client.

And then they fired us.

By fax machine.

If you're crazy about a team, they say you "bleed" the team colors. I went to the University of South Florida so I bleed green and gold, but in the 1990s I bled Mitsubishi red. Everyone at Zimmerman did. And what a run we had: In just over three years under our advertising leadership, we took Mitsubishi Motors North America from 136,000 annual sales to over a quarter million—nearly double their business. By anyone's standard, we were doing a hell of a job. But then came the change in management.

One of the hard facts of business is that people in charge get to do what they want, especially when they first take the reins. They don't always act predictably or even logically, and sometimes they don't even do what's best for the bottom line. When the new CEO took over at Mitsubishi, he put his personal stamp on the company by replacing key partners, starting with the advertising agency. It didn't matter that we were the best in the industry. We weren't *his* advertising agency, and that was the only thing that mattered. As was his privilege, he cut us loose.

By fax machine, no less.

We didn't screw up; we got screwed over. But there's a big difference: If something is your fault, you can fix it. If it's not your fault, all you can do—all you *should* do—is move on. To do anything else is to begin the descent into failure of the permanent kind, which is abandoning your goal.

When Mitsubishi dropped us, I was disappointed and angry, but I refused to throw a pity party about it. I didn't let anyone in my company do that, either. We knew the truth. There had been nothing missing in our approach. We were fired for political reasons, nothing more. It happened to us, and it will happen to you too.

If there isn't anyone outperforming you, or anyone smarter than you or faster than you, then don't sweat it. You're going to be sorely tempted to recalculate your position from the point of view of the person—the irrational person—who let you go. Resist the temptation. You'll be chasing ghosts.

The Mitsubishi decision, in one moment, lost us 40 percent of our business.

I could have let it wreck me. I could have crumbled under the weight of a hefty payroll to meet and serious obligations to answer. How did I bounce back? I chose to rise above the circumstances and stay focused on my goal.

I knew that I had to get back out there, find more business, and work harder. No way was I going to let this beat me. I don't like to lose, and I do not quit—not then and not now. Not ever. Neither should you.

JZ's CHAPTER TIPS

» Don't beat yourself up over mistakes.

» Determine the cause of a mistake, and
  make a plan so you don't do it again.

» Don't invest any more of your time, your
  thoughts, and your energy in a mistake.

PART IV

THE TROPHY GENERATION VERSUS PEOPLE WHO ACTUALLY DO THINGS

GIVING EVERYBODY A TROPHY DOESN'T CREATE WINNERS. IT JUST MAKES MORE LOSERS.

CHAPTER 18

Have you ever seen that TV show *The Biggest Loser*? It's about a bunch of people trying to lose a ton of weight in a big hurry. I have a better idea for that show. It ought to be pictures of everybody who went to high school and college in the last few decades, because nearly every one of them is potentially a real-life biggest loser—and it has nothing to do with stepping on the scale.

If you have grown up in the last twenty or thirty years, you are an official member of what I call the "Trophy Generation," and that's not good. How we came to this sad state is no mystery. All parents want what's best for their children. But somewhere along the way, recent generations have lost sight of the fact that achievers learn to achieve because early in life they experience defeat.

In other words, we learn to succeed as adults because, as children, we learn what it's like to fail.

Many of you now in early adulthood have been coddled your entire lives. You were taught that you are perfect "just the way you are." Adults didn't tell you how to improve what you were doing, and they didn't dare tell you that you were doing something wrong. Instead, they said that you were just doing things "your own way," which they said was perfect. Being a kid, you believed that.

This was and is a destructive force in your life.

Instead of letting you experience the consequences of your mistakes, they gave you a trophy. And for what? For nothing. When I go to the sports fields today with my kids, at the end of the season everybody gets a trophy. At a lot of kids' ball games, they don't even keep score! They just run around the bases, and at the end, all the kids get a cookie and a pat on the head, and they hear that everyone is a winner. How in the world does that teach anybody to try harder or to do his best?

If everybody who shows up is already a winner, why show up at all?

From that perspective, a trophy is worth nothing. And that's the world of the Trophy Generation—which is no way to prepare for real life.

I have heard all the excuses: *What about their self-esteem?* If you declare someone a winner, all the other kids are going to feel like losers! Wrong! You want to know the real problem? Kids are being raised by moms and dads so unaware of how the world actually works that they wouldn't recognize reality if it bit them on the behind.

Everything in life involves competition, which means there will always be winners and losers. This used to be common sense. But today that observation has become a rare insight, because so many softheaded people have come to believe that losing is "dangerous" and therefore, shouldn't be allowed.

I say, "Bullshit." Losing builds character. Everybody loses at times—and it's good for you. Losing has inspired me to improve myself, change my plan, and work harder. That's why competition has such value. I wouldn't be a success today, if I hadn't experienced losing along the way, unlike members of the Trophy Generation, who have been taught the opposite.

These kids, who've been insulated from the experience of losing, are starting life with a handicap more damaging than almost any other. Blame the parents— you bet I'll say that!—who have willingly set aside common sense for the weak comfort of a soft society. These allegedly responsible adults have refused to teach self-discipline and self-control.

Labeling everybody a "winner" doesn't make everybody a winner, and it certainly doesn't prepare anyone for the competitive real world we live in. It just deprives the losers of the opportunity to get better. Labeling everybody a "winner" imparts a false sense of achievement and implies that the hard work of true winners has no more value than the zero effort put forth by the rest.

It makes me angry. Allegedly responsible adults are teaching that mediocrity is something to aspire to! The lesson kids hear over and over is that the quality of your work has nothing to do with your reward.

That is not real life! And I hope you know the difference.

Go out and earn your next trophy by driving yourself to be better than everybody else. Deserve it because of a relentless commitment to be the absolute best.

It's time to abandon your place in the Trophy Generation!

JZ's CHAPTER TIPS

» Winners are recognized for talent and effort. Losers must try harder next time.

» Insulation from defeat was and is a destructive force in your life.

» Competition quickly and efficiently shows us what we are good at and where we need to improve.

» Go out and earn your next trophy. Earn it by driving yourself to be better than everybody else.

QUIT BEING AN ENTITLED LITTLE PRINCE OR PRINCESS FROM THE TROPHY GENERATION AND EMBRACE REALITY.

CHAPTER 19

The members of the Trophy Generation nurse Pollyannaish expectations about the world and what it takes to succeed. If you're in that group, it's time to break away from the mentality of entitlement. Those unrealistic ideas will kneecap your ability to achieve.

Your expectations have to line up with the way the world really is, not the way so many inexperienced mentors and uninformed peers have told you it's supposed to be. You need more than attitude to navigate reality. You need practical knowledge, self-discipline, skill, and a well-honed instinct for survival.

Reality has a way of issuing a clear verdict on your efforts. In the ad business it's pretty simple. I pitch clients, and if I don't produce enough winning pitches, I cannot pay my bills. That's a rock-bottom fact, and no pats on the head will change it. In real life, I'm competing against everybody else who wants the same things I do, and the spoils go only to those who are the best at what they do. Not everybody gets a trophy at the end of the day.

I'm fine with that, and you should be too. In fact, you should take that as good news about the path you're on: Competition is the great equalizer because it's based far more on performance than on personality, and your performance is something within your power to improve. Unless you're dealing with people who put their prejudices above profits, all that matters is how well your work stacks up against someone else's.

If my competitors and I pitch ten clients, and my competitors lose out to me every time, they should realize that my energy and ideas must have been better than theirs, and that's what led to my success. A wise competitor will look closely at what I'm doing and try to outsmart or outperform me using his or her own skills. Members of the Trophy Generation will look for answers everywhere else. That is too bad for them and a little ironic, too, because the areas they are ignoring are the only ones that can help them and the only ones they can quantifiably improve.

The Trophy Generation has been raised to believe that there's no difference between first, second, and last place. They've been spoiled by parents, teachers, coaches, and other people with good intentions and dream-world unrealistic ideas. But each of you princes and princesses will have to adjust to a reality that goes against most of what you've been taught. Second place may have won you a trophy before, but it sure won't get you one now.

I have a prescription for you: Wake up.

It's time to put away your juvenile expectations and start thinking like that rarest of modern commodities, a grown-up. Tell yourself this:

I'm going to be the very best I can be, and there's only one way to do it. I'm going to work harder than everybody else, and I am going to do whatever it takes. I'm going to set goals and lay out a path by which to achieve them, and I'm going to review my progress toward those goals every day. Whatever the rest of the world thinks my job is, I know that my real work—my lifetime career—is to make myself better and smarter every day and to go to bed each night closer to success than when I awoke that morning.

If I fail to discipline myself to do all that, I am not going to be a success in life.

And if I go back to acting like a spoiled little prince or princess from the Trophy Generation, I am absolutely done.

You can lie to yourself about the way the world works. You can lie to other people. You can be the most convincing liar in the whole world. But sooner rather than later, the truth will manifest itself.

JZ's CHAPTER TIPS

» The adults of the Trophy Generation must understand that the entitlement they cling to is the very thing that is hindering them.

» Reality has a way of always issuing a clear verdict.

» Recognize reality—then realign your expectations.

» Commit to improving yourself each and every day. Go to bed every night smarter than when you awoke.

» Parents and coaches hear this: Stop leagues from rewarding children with trophies that they have not earned and don't deserve.

» There is only one first place.

THE INSPIRATION OF
DESPERATION.

CHAPTER 20

So now you know you're not quite as special as everybody said you were. Boo hoo, big news. Thank me later.

But part of you is still hanging on to that notion. There is always someone who's special. Why not you, right?

Okay, I'll throw you a bone. You *are* special. Seriously! You're special because you are one of the few folks in the world who now understands that the Trophy Generation's view of the world is nonsense. Unfortunately, that won't get you out of the hard work it takes to achieve the success you want.

Sure, you've seen Mark Zuckerberg, Steve Jobs, and Bill Gates quit school and become billionaires. But look a little closer.

Those three weren't your ordinary college quitters. Zuckerberg and Gates were intellectual superstars before they arrived as freshmen, superior to many people already at the top of their fields. And they didn't walk away from some third-rate school that you've heard about in an infomercial on late-night TV. They both had been attending Harvard! But these two men turned out to be the rare individuals, for whom Harvard had little to offer. As for Jobs, he was enrolled at Reed College, a school that turns out more PhDs per year than MIT. He didn't quit to watch TV and drink beer. He stopped attending the classes he signed up for so he could slip into *other* classes that would give him the skills he knew he needed in industrial design and electronics. Those experiences and instructors were unavailable anywhere else. And when he dropped out, it was not to find himself. He left to exercise his unusual skills in a rare marketplace opportunity.

Unless you have singular talent and are already putting it to productive and profitable use, you are not the Zuckerberg-Gates-Jobs brand of dropout. That's not the worst news in the world. Being ordinary has its merits. Ordinary people know what it's like to work hard only to come crashing back to earth. And such a spectacular setback can open the door to spectacular success.

What's the most important thing that Henry Ford, Walt Disney, Domino's Pizza founder Tom Monaghan, and boxer-entrepreneur George Foreman have in common? If you're like most people, you'll say that all four became multimillionaires. (Actually, Ford and Disney became billionaires.) It's true that these men attained historic financial success, but that's not the most important life experience they share.

The most important thing these men share is that, at some point in their lives, all four went bankrupt.

For each, their profound ambitions came head to head with profound frustration. That's a powerful, combustible combination that can derail a life permanently. But in ambitious people who refuse to give up, it can have the opposite effect.

For these men, desperation yielded an explosion of creativity, energy, and commitment beyond any they had ever known. When it was do-or-die time, and all might have been lost, they didn't fold. They executed the best work of their lives.

They experienced the inspiration of desperation.

So my challenge to the Trophy Generation is this: When you're scared shitless, do something about it.

Right now many of you are much too comfortable to be truly desperate. You depend on others. You don't know what it's like to do without. You have not embraced genuine self-reliance.

Take chances—informed chances. Don't be afraid to miss a few meals. It is time to get desperate. Once you start living like it's all on you, I predict that you will know greater satisfaction on the road to success.

Many people are going through tough times, not only in the United States but also in the rest of the world. You are not the only one who may be dealt some bad cards. Are you going to feel sorry for yourself, or are you going to put your desperation to good use?

However terrible you think your circumstances are, there's always someone in a worse position, someone who will have to climb a little farther, overcome a little more, and suffer a little longer than you will.

For every woman who wants a promotion, there's another woman who just wants a job.

For every man who wants to own a business, there's another who just wants to be a part of one.

For every person who wants a vacation home, there's another who just wants a roof over his head.

I write this not so you will feel sorry for other people. I'm writing to say that desperation touches everyone, and it differs only by degree.

What you need to remember is that the inspiration of desperation can propel you toward your goal no matter where you are on the economic ladder, no matter what your situation in life. What counts is how you deal with desperation. Success is still up to you. How badly do you want it?

For some people, tough times are a reason to give up and scream for help. These people are waiting for their uncle to arrange a job interview, for the government to write a check, for Mom and Dad to swoop in and fix everything, or for the winning lottery number to come up.

For other people, tough times are a reason to get serious, to pay closer attention, to raise their game a notch or three, to finally become so dissatisfied with their surroundings that they simply have to take massive action and change their own world.

You have to do that, because no one else is going to change it for you.

If you really do admire people like Mark Zuckerberg, Steve Jobs, or Bill Gates, remember that none of them were wait-and-see-what-happens kind of guys. They all took hard knocks: Jobs lost his company, but he got it back and made it bigger than ever. Gates became embroiled in a corporate life-or-death struggle with IBM and won. Zuckerberg is presently navigating the rapidly evolving world of social media that could drive him to even greater achievement or capsize his company. Whether he wins or loses this particular battle, it would be unwise to bet against Zuckerberg in the long march toward achievement.

Sooner or later, desperation is going to visit, and a decision will be forced upon you. Be prepared—mentally prepared—to choose wisely. Successful people respond to desperation with action. Do you have the power in you to do that? Let me answer for you: Yes! But only you can choose to tap into it.

Steve Jobs once told a group of graduates to "Stay hungry. Stay foolish."[5] Here's what I will add to his excellent advice: Stay desperate.

---

5. Steve Jobs, "How to Live before You Die," Commencement address, Stanford University, filmed June 2005. TED video, 15:04, http://www.ted.com/talks/steve _jobs_how_to_live_before_you_die.

JZ's CHAPTER TIPS

» A spectacular setback can open the door to spectacular success.

» The inspiration of desperation can propel you toward your goal, no matter where you are on the economic ladder, no matter your situation in life.

» Stay hungry. Stay foolish. Stay desperate.

PART V

THERE'S ONLY ONE FINISH LINE—DON'T LOSE SIGHT OF IT

OUTCOME BEATS OUTPUT
EVERY SINGLE TIME.

CHAPTER 21

If you want to succeed—and since you're reading my book I believe that you do—you have to remain focused at all times on outcome. The bottom line, the real goal, must be the one thing that matters to you in the end.

Maybe you work in a convenience store, and you want to work in an office instead.

Maybe you work in an office, and you want to work outside!

Maybe you want to live overseas, or learn to fly, or own your own home, or start your own business.

Whether you're a hairdresser who wants to start her own shop or a manager who wants to be CEO—or anything else you can think of—you must know what you want, identify it clearly, and stay focused on the path to get there.

But get this straight: The path to success is filled with temptations and distractions that can feel as if *they* were what you were aiming at all along. The amusement and pleasure of those distractions can replace your goal, and you will hardly realize it happened.

If life is a highway, you're going to have to ignore a whole lot of eye-catching roadside attractions on the way to wherever you're going. You will need to train your mind to recognize the goal as the only prize worth having. You must steel yourself to see the efforts and accolades along the way for what they are—tools and stepping-stones toward that prize.

How can you focus on your goal if you can't articulate what it is? You can't. So the first thing you need to do is put your goal into simple words. Take a walk and consider what you really want. Have a conversation with someone you trust. If you want to sit down with a pad and paper, that's fine. Do whatever it takes. But in the end, you need to have a sentence that you carry around in your head that summarizes your desired outcome—the thing you are trying to achieve:

- "I'm going to start my own business."

- "I'm going to own my own home."

- "I'm going to earn a promotion to vice president."

- "I'm going to save $25,000."

- "I'm getting a master's degree."

You are going to need a precise intention and some serious strength to reach your goal, and you're going to feel the temptation to bask in the glory of intermediate achievements. But at every one of those little victories, remind yourself that the outcome— that sentence you memorized—is all that matters. The stepping-stones and the skills that you have mastered along the way are no more than that. The real prize is all that matters.

To help you keep perspective, let's go even further in adjusting your outlook. In your mind, you must degrade and devalue those intermediate steps. Reduce them to something as disposable as grocery bags.

Here's what I mean.

If you want to get your groceries home from the store, you have to put them in bags. Those sacks are vital, but it would be silly to brag about them. All your family cares about is that there's food in the refrigerator. The value of those bags begins and ends with making that possible.

Look at every achievement along your own path as a shopping bag—a simple tool that helps you achieve the important outcome.

You want to live in Spain, so you learn to speak Spanish. Speaking Spanish is a shopping bag. It's an achievement, but it's an *intermediate* achievement on the path to your real goal.

You want to be a CEO, so you earn a degree in business. Earning that degree is a shopping bag. It's also an achievement, but an intermediate one.

It would be easy to bask in the glory of either of those achievements, but basking in the *intermediate* glory does nothing to get you closer to your desired outcome.

Learning to speak Spanish was output along the way. The outcome is getting to Spain.

Say you're a chef, and your goal is to serve the best home-style dinners in town. That's a reasonable thing to shoot for, and it will take commitment and hard work to achieve it. Start with your clearly stated goal: "I want to be the best at creating great-tasting home-style dinners!"

But what if you "fall in love" with something else along the way? Impossible, you say? Not so fast. What if you start working less on the food and more on building a state-of-the-art kitchen to impress your peers and getting the "right" kind of customers to be seen in your restaurant? What if you spend less effort on the food and more time trying to get coverage in the newspaper? Pretty soon your attention has wandered far away from your original goal, and your customers will wander away too. They were coming for the great cuisine, not to *ooh* and *aah* over your fancy kitchen or eat second-rate food in first-rate company.

You need a high-quality kitchen, but that's not an end in itself.

You need the right branding, but that's not your sole intended destination.

You need publicity, but that is not entirely your original goal.

If you fail to deliver on your goal, nobody gives a damn about how much you impressed yourself and others along the way. Failure is failure, and distractions are off-ramps to failure.

Stay focused on the overall outcome, not the intermediate output. Many would-be achievers fall in that trap, and that's the last we hear of them. It happens in every industry, every day.

There's only one finish line. Don't lose sight of it. The prize is the destination, not the intermediate output or the interim pats on the back.

It's the checkered flag that matters, not how you drive.

It's the touchdown that matters, not how pretty the pass is.

It's the victory that matters, not the kudos you picked up along the way.

Outcome, not output, is your goal.

JZ's CHAPTER TIPS

» Whoever you are and whatever your goal, you must know what you want, identify it clearly, and stay on track to get there.

» The path to success is filled with temptations and distractions.

» If you fail to deliver on your goal, nobody will care how much you impressed yourself and others along the way.

» There is only one finish line. Don't ever lose sight of it.

TOOTHLESS LIONS.

CHAPTER 22

Outcome—achieving the great goal at the end—is what matters. Output—the trivial, ego-stroking success along the way—doesn't matter at all. I've succeeded in my industry in part because I remember that when so many others forget it. I focus relentlessly on every goal I seek, and I never accept defeat no matter what it takes to win. This is what I know to be the commonsense path to success.

Believe it or not, that is one of the things that makes me the "bad boy" of the advertising industry.

You know what? I like it that way.

If you suspect that I have a reputation for being

controversial, you're right. It's well earned too. I *am* controversial. I make people uncomfortable. Fine with me. I'm a maverick.

But what about everyone else? I meet a fair number of people who can't reach their goals and are genuinely puzzled as to why. These are intense, ambitious, creative people with unique skills, but they've lost sight of something important.

These people would be more successful if they stayed focused on outcome over output, if they kept their eyes on bottom-line success for their clients instead of seeking applause for their own work. Here's an example from my industry.

A round-trip airline ticket to France costs about $1,500 for coach. (You'd like to go first class? Add a zero to that.) A week in a five-star hotel is about $4,000. Food and drink and incidentals? Call that $2,000. Add it up and a very nice week to enjoy the best France has to offer will set you back about $10,000.

Let's say you run an advertising firm, and you send a dozen of your "superstars" on this trip for a week. That's more than a hundred grand—a ton of money to anyone, whether you have a lot in the bank or a little.

Plus that makes a week that your best people aren't working for your clients.

Why in the world would you do that?

In the advertising industry, that French getaway is not some super-special, once-in-a-lifetime reward for a job well done. It's an annual expense, an annual *business* expense, believe it or not.

Every June, moguls from the advertising industry gather in Cannes, on the famous French Riviera, to honor the best work by the artists, writers, and directors—the "creatives"—of the industry. Similar to the Academy Awards, this party is called the Cannes Lions International Festival of Creativity, and the top prize is the Lion. (By the way, if you win one, it isn't free. You have to pay $200 to have the thing shipped it back to the States. Not only does it cost a fortune to attend the event, you have to pay to get your prize back home!)

How do you win a Lion? You come up with what a panel of judges decides is the most creative jingle or TV ad or billboard. They add new categories every year, so it's getting hard not to win one, assuming you are willing to fork out the cash to participate in the first place.

Think about that: We're talking about a trophy for creating an ad that other advertisers like—a prize not for creating success for the clients who pay your salary but for impressing your peers and competitors!

Did your ad bring new customers to the client's portfolio? That doesn't matter.

Did it increase the client's sales? That doesn't matter, either.

Did it lead to record revenue for the client? One more time: It doesn't matter, not at Cannes.

All the things that *do* matter to a business don't count for the judges at Cannes. Hell, your client could be out of business, and you can still win! Advertising history is filled with cool-looking ads from long-gone companies. Yet this prize, which is not based in any way on how effective the ad actually is, is one of the highest honors in my industry.

So when I meet someone who has a Lion on his shelf, I have to ask: *How the hell does that help the guy who paid for it?*

The best and brightest from all over the world invest months and months of work trying to win one of these trophies, when what they ought to be doing is figuring out ways to help their clients succeed.

These "creatives" are focused on the output—pretty ads—instead of the outcome, which is getting more business for the client. The outcome—that bottom line—is exactly what the client is paying for. That's all that matters.

Last time I checked, my bank sent me a statement accounting for dollars and cents, not trophies and plaques.

Chasing a trophy for creativity is a betrayal of the people who foot the bill for advertising. It's a spectacular waste of time, money, and real talent that could have been spent working toward your client's goal. If these guys were basketball players, they'd be fighting over who has the coolest sneakers instead of trying to get the ball in the basket!

I'm not saying these creative types aren't talented. I'm not saying their work doesn't have some sort of artistic merit, because it often does. And the ads themselves may actually be effective. It's possible!

What I am saying is that as soon as the goal and the focus shift from getting results to simply making a trophy ad, it's game over.

So many of the big shots I see in my industry are celebrating the work itself, not what the work actually achieved for their client. These people are celebrating *output*, not *outcome*.

They are delighting in the applause for creative advertising, not client profitability. They're celebrating themselves instead of what they achieved for their clients! Creativity is nice, but what the client pays for is *results*.

Last time I checked, from my view at one of the most successful advertising firms in the world, clients are more interested in bottom-line results than they are in paying for yacht parties in the south of France.

You know what my bookshelf has on it? Books. There's no Cannes Creative Lion up there, no Clio Award, no One Show Pencils. My trophy shelf is empty, but my desk is piled high with daily reports from every one of my clients. And do you know what's in those reports? The dollars-and-cents details of what my agency did for them that day, what we've done for them so far in total, and what we're going to do for them tomorrow.

There's only one opinion that matters besides my own, and that is the opinion of my client.

I don't care about arranging prizes on my shelves,

and I don't need my competitors standing around clapping for me. My reward is my clients' success— and that is measured in dollars and cents, end of story. In business, that's what matters.

So what about you and your ultimate goal?

Whatever you are trying to achieve in life, keep your eye on what matters. When you work for somebody, they're not paying you to impress *somebody else*. They're paying you to impress *them*. Keep your eye on the ultimate goal, and don't mistake the little victories along the way for the big prize at the finish line.

Make no mistake. It takes less effort to settle for a quick and easy victory in the moment than it does to keep working for that long-term goal. Never choose immediate gratification over the hard work of patience, determination, and rejection of the temptation to take the easy way out. Immediate gratification is the distraction.

Do not be distracted and led astray by shiny baubles. Stay focused on the ultimate prize, that of your own success. Quit chasing trophies. Start pursuing dreams, and do so with determination, focus, and ferocity. That's how you turn them into reality.

JZ's CHAPTER TIPS

» Successful people focus on outcome.

» Successful people keep their eyes on bot-tom-line success for their clients, instead of seeking applause for their own work.

» When people have a shelf full of awards, you should ask yourself if they are in busi-ness to win awards for themselves or to win business for their clients.

» When the goal shifts from getting results to simply winning a trophy along the way, failure is at hand.

» Creativity is nice, but what matters is the result.

» Immediate gratification can be the distraction.

» Pursue your dreams with determination, focus, and ferocity. That's how you turn them into reality.

IF YOU WANT TO BUILD A RAILROAD, SOMETIMES YOU HAVE TO BUILD A STEEL MILL FIRST.

CHAPTER 23

More and more often today, people say that compared to other nations, there is nothing special about America. They imagine that the comment makes them seem open-minded, inclusive, and wise. *There are plenty of countries besides this one where people work hard, do well, and find success*, they say, and in a way they're right. But at a deeper level, what they're saying is that there's nothing that profoundly sets our nation apart.

And in that they're wrong. They're cleaving to an opinion that blinds them to a simple reading of history, a conclusion intuitively obvious to the casual observer.

Every country on the face of the earth was founded for god or king or treasure, for ethnicity or race or power, or the prideful rush of bloody conquest—except for America.

America was founded explicitly as a place where people could come to pursue their dreams, whatever those dreams may be. The Founding Fathers envisioned a place where people could live life to the fullest, as any individual defines it, limited only by their willingness to work for it. Ours is a nation with the word "happiness" in its Declaration of Independence—"Life, Liberty and the pursuit of Happiness." That's an insane idea, especially for the eighteenth century! Here's a country created not to impress a king or to lay claim to a fortune, but simply as a place where people could flee oppression great or small and declare, *Here is where I will make my own happiness with my own hands, with my own intellect, as I alone see fit, without interference from others.*

This isn't difficult to understand, and it's not a matter of opinion but a matter of fact. You're telling me America isn't exceptional? You obviously haven't thought much about the point. Does America have flaws? Of course it does, just like every other country. But American *exceptionalism* as I've described it here, has nothing to do with those flaws. Pouting and breath-holding from academic types who haven't achieved anything won't change the truth that many of us know not just from books but also from hard-won experience: The United States stands as the singular creation of a laboratory for progress, opportunity, and self-fulfillment toward the greater progress of mankind everywhere.

America was founded on the truth that you have the right to pursue your own dreams. The fact that the struggle to extend that truth to every man and woman is still ongoing is not an indictment of America but rather a testament to the virtues of the people who live here. No other nation is built on that idea—none whatsoever. This is a rare and special place.

And particularly rare are those who are able to recognize and capitalize on the many opportunities America provides to its citizens.

Many of the people who came here or came of age in the eighteenth and nineteenth centuries arrived with a grand vision to be the best they could be—to become entrepreneurs, creators, and inventors and to build the industrial foundation for a young nation entering a brand-new age of achievement. They assembled an infrastructure, not just factories for their own profit but also pathways for widespread trade and commerce that made possible the wonders of the modern age: the airplane, the telephone, the automobile, the electrical grid, the interstate highway system, the television, the computer, and the Internet. Not only that, they also established a standard of living that would become the envy of the world. More than 300 million Americans live in this land of plenty, a place that kings of a century ago would have considered lavish.

None of this happened spontaneously. It started with a few great men who refused to think of themselves as average; they were ambitious titans of industry who dreamed beyond the limits of the age.

One of those giants was Cornelius Vanderbilt, a man of such amazing accomplishments that the world-famous university he created and that bears his name was a later-in-life chapter of his story, almost an afterthought. Vanderbilt started his first business as a teenager. He ran a ferry service and, over time, built it into a steamboat line and eventually into an oceangoing transportation company.

Steamboats may not sound like a big deal today,

but before and in the early years of the railroad age, they were that era's equivalent of our jet airliners. As his steamboats began to compete with and complement America's first railroads, Vanderbilt entered that business too. In fact, he became one of the fathers of the U.S. railroad industry. In the decades before the Civil War, Vanderbilt wasn't just becoming a part of some well-established industry. He was *creating* an industry and doing it almost from scratch. At the start of his journey, Vanderbilt had a lower net wealth than nearly anyone reading this book.

J.P. Morgan went into banking about the same time Vanderbilt was building a fortune in steamboats and railways. Morgan was one of the first men to take a step-by-step approach to transforming failing businesses into profitable ones. In this way he was the equivalent of the modern "turnaround artist," a businessperson who buys a business that is failing and restructures it to preserve jobs, opportunity, and profit. (By the way, many people who do this kind of work today are portrayed as greedy profiteers. What critics refuse to acknowledge is that when a business is on a downward slide to failure, you can restructure the company and save some of the jobs, or let it rot and lose them all. But perhaps I'm being too hard on these critics, few of whom have had to meet a payroll, or make the hard choices that affect their employees' livelihoods and incomes. After all, it's easier to portray business leaders as evil than it is to study economics.)

As a banker, Morgan had so many connections across so many industries that he had access to a lot of opportunities, which is another way of saying that he had an excellent vantage point from which to recognize the greatest needs of nineteenth-century America. He had the experience and ability to recognize which opportunities were promising and which would lead to a dead end.

Morgan made some important, amazing, and influential choices. As a partner with Charles M. Schwab (no relation to today's financial Schwab) and Andrew Carnegie in the founding of United States Steel, Morgan not only contributed to tremendous railroad expansion, he also established Pittsburgh, Pennsylvania, as the heart of what would become the industrial Northeast for more than a century. U.S. Steel was the first billion-dollar company in the world, eclipsing in size even the railroads it helped to launch and grow.

Morgan invested in a lot of things and took up

a common cause with others who shared his ambition, men who dreamed of creating great change in the world and creating interesting, outsized lives for themselves. Morgan backed Thomas Edison to bring electricity to every home in America. Not long after, Morgan founded General Electric. In a little less than twenty-five years, Morgan's company organized or underwrote forty-two major corporations, including International Harvester and AT&T.

Then there was the co-founder of Standard Oil, John D. Rockefeller, the man who created the modern oil industry. Morgan may have founded the first company worth more than a billion dollars, but Rockefeller was the first individual to be personally worth a billion. Adjusted for inflation, Rockefeller was the wealthiest man in history. Before the widespread availability of commercial electricity, he made a fortune selling kerosene. How did he distribute it? Using the railways of Cornelius Vanderbilt!

These men were overachievers, and I mean that as high praise. They not only provided jobs and opportunity for other Americans, but they also raised the quality of life for everyone. Each man's great achievements helped make possible the success of their contemporaries and the life-changing industries they created. Morgan's steel went into Vanderbilt's railroad. Vanderbilt's railroad carried Rockefeller's kerosene. Rockefeller's kerosene was replaced by Edison's lightbulb, which was financed by Morgan's banking, which grew, in part, thanks to Carnegie's steel business. Around and around and around it goes.

There's much to learn about your own pursuit of success from the way these American giants did it.

They never had a final goal, just a next goal.

And although they became spectacularly wealthy men, they were driven not only by profit but also by the desire to achieve even greater things. They dreamed big. They embraced fear and never ran from it. They were never intimidated.

Their directions in life were chosen on the basis of what they could imagine, not by what the world told them was possible. They did not tether their dreams to anyone else's limits. Conventional wisdom meant nothing to them. If they could identify a challenge, they believed they could meet that challenge—and they did.

Even though they did not have the advantages of the modern world that we enjoy, their successes still dwarf anything achieved by anyone since. They created the infrastructure that made possible the rise of cities, startling discoveries, innovative industries, and entirely new ways of life.

Whatever they encountered in their futures arose in large part from the hard work they did in their own day. They knew that each project, each achievement, was not an end in itself. Each effort could eventually become a link in a larger chain of achievements or a stepping-stone toward something that had yet to be dreamed, something that would be possible tomorrow only because of work done well today. I like to think they might have said this to themselves: *If you want to build a railroad tomorrow, you have to build a steel mill today.*

You don't have to aspire to create a new industry, as Vanderbilt or Rockefeller did. But you do have to work as hard as they did.

I'm not kidding.

You have to be as serious as they were, as ambitious as they were, and as insanely committed as they were. You can do that! They were intelligent, and so are you. All the rest is a matter of will.

What kind of person will you be? Our nation was

not built on mediocrity. Your own bright future will not be built on mediocrity, either.

I have no time for the critics and complainers who don't like the way I do things, and neither should you. As Teddy Roosevelt said, "It is not the critic who counts; not the man who points out . . . where the doer of deeds could have done them better. The credit belongs to the man who is actually in the arena, whose face is marred by dust and sweat and blood . . . "[6]

Aim high: Model your life after the consuming passion of these great men of industry. They had vision, and vision is not seeing what is. Vision is seeing what could be.

---

6. Theodore Roosevelt, "Citizenship in a Republic," speech delivered at the Sorbonne in Paris, France, April 23, 1910, http://www.theodore-roosevelt.com/trsorbonnespeech.html.

JZ's CHAPTER TIPS

» Successful people choose their paths through life on the basis of what they can imagine, not on what the world tells them is possible.

» If you want to build a railroad tomorrow, you have to build a steel mill today.

» Our nation was not built on mediocrity. Your own bright future will not be built on mediocrity, either.

» Vision is seeing what could be.

WILL THE REAL JORDAN ZIMMERMAN PLEASE STAND UP?

CHAPTER 24

Here's a surprise: There's more than one "you."

There's the you that your buddies see. There's the you that your spouse or your boyfriend or girlfriend sees. There's the you from school, the you from business, the you around your parents, even the you that you alone get to see, when you make those vital decisions that determine the course of your life.

If you're trying to lead your life fearlessly as you go for your goal, "you" needs some additional attention. There's usually a difference between how you are perceived and how you would most like to be perceived. It's time to close that gap. It's time for the real "you" to stand up. It's time to think of yourself as a brand.

You may not realize it, but, as you go through life, you become a brand and for good or bad, a few stand-out characteristics come to define you. They give people an automatic feeling about you, just like they do for Papa John's and Nissan and Boston Market and White Castle and so many other corporate images I've helped to shape.

Creating a personal brand starts as soon as you're old enough to interact with other people with more than drool and bouncy-baby handclaps. Think about yourself in school, or remember someone you knew then. Was this person always ready for class, with homework done and pencils sharpened? Did he get good grades, and was it because he was smart or because he kissed ass? Was she fun to be around or was she a jerk? Did he always "kill it" on tests? Was she a jock or a brain or a nerd, or some combination of those identities? Did he put his name on every extracurricular sign-up sheet, or did he laugh at the people who did? Did she do just enough to get by, or did she turn in perfect homework plus all the extra credit? When you saw this person coming, were you glad, or did you walk the other way?

School, work, community, whatever the situation—how you behave in those environments becomes your character, personality, and brand. For better or worse, you are a brand, a personal brand. What's more, you always have been. It's the basis on which both friends and strangers decide whether to hire you or help you or ignore you.

So far, your brand has just "happened" to you without any planning. You're going to change that. It's time to take control of that brand, to take an active role in how everybody else sees you.

Here's how this journey began in my life. Early on, I asked myself, *Will the real Jordan Zimmerman please stand up?*

Where I grew up in New Jersey, I built myself as a good brand, and by that I mean I conducted myself in such a way that the kids in my school knew I was a friendly kid, a good student, a guy with a quick wit and a funny comeback, and a better athlete than opponents expected. When the name Jordan Zimmerman came up, teachers and students knew what they were getting. Then, in my teenage years, my parents moved us to Florida. As soon as I walked into my new school, Piper High, I saw all these new kids, and I thought, *Hey, wait a minute. I'm not a brand anymore!*

Then I thought again: *Oh, yes, I am still a brand. My new audience just doesn't have brand awareness yet.*

I realized this wasn't a problem but an opportunity! So I said to myself, *They may not know any of the good things about me, but they don't know any of the things that I don't like about me, either. This is a fresh start! So is there anything about the Jordan brand that I want to change?*

I was afforded something life rarely offers, a do-over.

I was already an ambitious young man, so this opportunity drove me to soul-searching. For the first time in my life, I thought hard about how I wanted to be perceived, not because I cared what people thought about me, but because their appropriate perception of the brand called Jordan could be of great use. In particular, I thought how those thoughts and feelings would help or hurt me in the things I needed to achieve as a high school student on the road to an advertising and marketing career. For instance, I would need teachers to give me recommendation letters for college. Teachers won't write those letters for just anybody, at least not a really good letter that can make a difference. So I asked myself, *What kind of student gets the best letter?*

The smart students get the good letters, but being smart isn't everything. Those letters go to the ones who stand out in a good way. The ones who show appreciation for what the teacher does. The ones who do more than the teacher expects.

Then I asked myself, *What kind of student does a university most readily accept?*

Again, it's more than just a smart student, though intelligence is vital. They want to see a well-rounded student, one who participates inside the classroom and out. One who shows self-determination and initiative. One who is a part of both the school and the community.

I examined my situation from every angle I could think of, from family life to friendships, athletics, my interests, my fears, and of course, my goals after college. I knew I could reach my goals faster if I leveraged my brand. As you see, I figured out: (1) what kind of brand—what kind of person—was most advantaged in this pursuit and (2) how I should behave so that people would see me in the appropriate way.

I formed new habits. I acted consciously and with

purpose. I disciplined myself to choose appreciation over disregard. I chose to exceed not only my expectations but also those of the people around me.

Some of these things I was already doing. Others, not so much. But now I was going to do them all.

My brand would be my behavior.

Your brand will be your behavior too.

Just as the real Jordan Zimmerman decided to stand up, the real you has to make that decision also.

Success is not a destination but a process and *a way of behaving*. It's what you choose to do every day. Your personal brand is exactly the same thing. Excellence is not something you pull out once in a while when it's convenient or momentarily helpful. Excellence is a way of life. "We are what we repeatedly do. Excellence, then, is not an act but a habit."[7]

We are what we repeatedly do.

That's how you build your personal brand. And here's some good news you weren't expecting: The harder you work toward something you want, the more that decision in your brain becomes the passion in your heart. The work comes easier when you're

---

7. Will Durant, *The Story of Philosophy: The Lives and Opinions of the World's Greatest Philosophers* (New York: Simon & Schuster, 1926).

driven by a love of what you're doing. Most successful people aren't driven by money and nothing else. The best are driven by passion for their goal.

The way you conduct yourself—behavior by both habit and will—is another piece of the puzzle in achieving success. Over time, the self-discipline that you have worked so hard to build spins chore into habit and habit into passion. At that point your motivation comes from your soul, from your deepest desire.

Excellence is a habit that turns into passion. Your brand is a reflection of that constant commitment.

So far, you have probably formed your brand by accident—by the sum total of how people perceive your behaviors, with no planning or intention on your part. Well, enough of that. It's time to redefine your brand to your own specifications. Identify a characteristic you want people to see in you, focus on three to five new and necessary behaviors that will bring it about, and then make those a part of your daily life. Get good at them, while constantly reevaluating the behaviors you need to reach your goal. Adjust accordingly. And stay on the path.

Your brand is the passion inside you. It's time for the real you to stand up!

JZ's CHAPTER TIPS

» We are what we repeatedly do.

» The harder you work toward something you want, the more that decision in your brain becomes the passion in your heart.

» Excellence is a habit that turns into passion. Your brand is a reflection of that constant commitment.

» Your brand is the passion inside you.

PART VI

START MAKING PROGRESS TODAY, NOT TOMORROW

IF YOU DON'T HAVE A GOAL, YOU DON'T HAVE A LIFE.

CHAPTER 25

It's true on the highway, and it's true in life: You cannot reach your destination if you don't know where you're going. If you don't have a goal in mind, you have something else to look forward to—regret.

It's never too late to find a goal, but it's never too early, either. Part of the reason so many people in their twenties, thirties, and beyond—maybe you—are so far behind in achieving their dreams is that no authority figure has ever shared with them how vital it is to have a dream or a goal or a lifetime destination.

I'm outraged over kids coming out of high school with no goals. High school has to be more than time spent preparing for nothing in particular. Whether we notice or not, high school prepares students for the next step in their life, and kids need to pick something and work toward it. High school is the time to start making a plan. That doesn't mean you can't change it later. Most kids will. But starting life without direction is a handicap no one needs.

Would you get on a plane with a pilot who didn't have a flight plan? Of course not. So why would you go to college without having a plan for what you want to do? Is something magical going to happen? That's not the way the world works. Kids should leave high school with a goal and head for a college that will help them reach that goal.

I found a goal earlier than most. I knew in eighth grade that I wanted to go into marketing and advertising. My son tells me that makes me weird. Maybe so, but take a look at my career and my company. If that's weird, then everybody should be so weird.

Did you ever wonder why so many people end up unhappy later in life? It's usually because they didn't choose a life for themselves. Life just "happened" to them. They took whatever came along, they settled for it, and then they wondered why they felt so dissatisfied and lousy day after day, year after year. I grew up hearing adults complaining about money and jobs, and my dad set me straight on why their lives turned out that way: "They're not unhappy because they want to be," he said. "They're unhappy because they took whatever life handed them, instead of making their own way."

If you don't have a goal, you are screwed. And even if you do have a goal, you have to pursue it and transform it from a dream into reality, or you're still screwed.

If you wake up every morning feeling like *there has to be more to life than this,* it's probably because you never chose a goal! You have to choose a goal and then differentiate yourself from the sea of sameness out there. Otherwise you'll never ever have success, and you'll be one of the people turning forty or fifty and lamenting *I wish I would have . . . I know I could have . . .*

There are fascinating stories in history about those who are born to wealth and make a wreck of their lives. The riches, the opportunity, the access, the advantages—all these end up wasted.

The lesson, though, is not that wealth corrupts. Yes, it *can* corrupt, but it doesn't have to. Wealthy people fail for the same reason poor people fail: the lack of a goal. A life without a point is pointless, and it very quickly begins to fall down around you! The rich just have more wealth to lose. They have further to fall. That's why we notice.

But every person who fails feels the same when he hits the ground.

Whatever you want to do with your life, choose a goal. It's okay if you change it later, but there's no excuse to put it off. Think of yourself as a great achiever, and then consider what great achievers do: They latch on to a vision of what is possible for themselves and sometimes for the whole world. They look beyond what is to what could be. They do whatever it takes to reach their goal.

Those people are champions, and as you have probably figured out by now the world is not running over with champions. It's full of men and women who stick to the path somebody else blazed. They don't go where *they* want to go. They go where they think they can get. Or worse, they bounce around with no goal at all, going where life takes them, instead of leading their own life as they themselves see fit.

The great majority of men and women talk a big game about how famous and important they'll be and how much money they'll have and how many houses and boats and islands they'll own—but those are the people who never produce, never achieve, never finish what they start. A lot of them never even get to the starting line!

Why is that? They never chose a goal.

You have to choose a goal. So do it.

JZ's CHAPTER TIPS

» You cannot reach your destination, if you don't know where you're going.

» It's never too late to choose a goal, but it's never too early, either.

» If you don't have a goal, you won't have a life. And even if you do have a goal, you have to pursue it and then transform that dream into reality, or you still won't have a life.

» Differentiate yourself in the sea of sameness.

» Every person who fails feels the same when he hits the ground.

» Great achievers have great vision. They look beyond what is to what could be.

FIND THE REAL PROBLEM.

CHAPTER 26

You've read enough of my book to know that the ball's in your court. To achieve your personal goal, you have to stay focused on it, no matter what distractions come your way. By focusing relentlessly on the future—throwing away the nonsense and distractions and shiny baubles that most people get lost in—the clarity that you earn will give you a way to see through other challenges in life.

Think of it this way: Examine every challenge that comes your way. And before you focus on solving a problem, be sure you know exactly what the problem is. Sometimes it will surprise you. This idea is at the heart of one of the most powerful techniques I use in my own business.

Since I work in advertising, I always assumed that ads are what people want when they come to me. But over time I began to look at that daily challenge in more detail. In particular, I started to put myself more and more in my clients' position. Start thinking like the people you're serving, and your perspective changes. That's the kind of insight careful thinking will give you. But back to my story.

I realized that I'd be serving my clients more effectively if I changed my focus to serving them holistically. By that I mean I wanted to look at their business as a whole. I had been focused on selling the client only what I had to offer; instead I decided to provide them with whatever it was they needed!

Here's an example. If you call somebody to put in new carpet in your house, and they see that the floor underneath has some broken places, the high-quality company won't just roll out their wares over the bad floor. First they'll help you find a way to fix the real problem. Only then will they put their carpet in place.

It ought to be the same way in every business. If someone comes in to buy whatever you sell, the first thing you ought to do is figure out what that person really needs.

But that doesn't happen too often. It's not because the businesspeople are trying to rip off their customers. It's because they didn't realize that the best way to do their job—both for the benefit of the client and their own professional future—is to provide the best answer for their client's needs, no matter what.

I realized that I could be of greater service to my clients if I identified their real problems, needs, and goals instead of just selling them ads.

You know that old saying, *If all you have is a hammer, every problem looks like a nail.* That's how most people do business. I create advertising, so every problem that I saw looked like a job for—*ta dah!*—advertising!

But not anymore, and I am proud that I realized so soon that I could do better. Using that focus guided me to success. I learned to think beyond my preconceived notions of any situation—beyond even the expectations of the potential client.

And from little acorns, big trees grow.

The insight that started out as my idea in my own company grew into a phenomenon across the advertising industry. Today it's known as Brandtailing.™ As a *CNN.com* story once put it, it turns out that companies want an approach that makes you buy their products.[8] Funny that something so obvious to you and me seems so foreign to so many others.

My approach is to identify the *real* problem and take that on in whatever way it requires, and only *then* to figure out the best advertising solution to follow. That's how we do it here at Zimmerman, and the outcome has been fantastic. One of the first companies we helped this way was Miami Subs, a great operation that sells sandwiches not only in Miami but all over Florida and as far away as Hawaii and South America.

When they came to us, their sales had been off for at least a year. The company thought the answer was a new campaign—just the sort of thing we provide. But after I took a look around their stores—and when I thought about my commitment to examine the client's needs from the ground up—I realized something else pretty fast.

These stores needed . . . how to put this nicely? Miami Subs didn't need a new ad campaign, not yet.

---

8. Ellen Neuborne, "Ads That Actually Sell Stuff," *CNN Money*, Business 2.0, June 1, 2004, http://money.cnn.com/magazines/business2/business2_archive/2004/06/01/370471/.

Miami Subs needed mops and brooms and elbow grease! The stores needed cleaning up, top to bottom. When we went in to deliver our "pitch," we didn't show up with what an advertising company usually brings— no storyboards, no video, no PowerPoint. Instead, we arrived with buckets and mops, and we told them: "We'll be glad to do an ad campaign for you, but what you need to do first is clean up your stores!"

We were candid with them, something unheard of in a lot of ad agencies. We explained that the condition of their stores was a lot of the reason why customers weren't coming in. Any ad campaign we would build would be far more successful if we fixed this fundamental problem first.

We knew this approach to a new client could go one of two ways: They could applaud us for taking a bold stand—giving them an unpleasant-to-hear assessment but one that could help turn around the trajectory of their sagging sales.

Or they could cut us off before we finished and throw us out on our asses.

We walked into a meeting of about eighty franchisees. For each of them, this business represented their livelihood. For many, it had been the fulfillment of the same kind of dream held by many of you who are reading this right now: to own their own business.

We had nothing but the very best intentions, but we also knew that people sometimes mistake honesty for disrespect. We were hoping these people weren't those kind of people.

So we showed up carrying buckets and mops. We didn't soften our story with compliments or pretty words. We chose to believe that they, too, thought that it's best to deal with the world as it is, not as we wish it would be. And we delivered our simple message. If you want to succeed, clean up your stores!

The meeting turned quiet—very quiet—for what felt like forever.

And then the questions started: "What do you mean? Why? Tell us more!"

These weren't angry questions. The people who owned Miami Subs wanted to know what in the world was so key to successful business that advertising people stopped talking about advertising, the very thing they make their own money with.

They simply weren't accustomed to dealing with an agency where the client really is the first priority. They weren't accustomed to candor and a sincerely shared enthusiasm for the health not of just the ad budget, but of the entire company.

They wanted to know who the hell we were, and what kind of people do what we had just done.

People who respect their clients, that's who.

At first glance, there may not seem to be much of a future in that approach—candor and tough straight talk. But doing things right, no matter how hard it may be, is where the most promising future is always found.

And that's a huge lesson for you: Successful people become successful by solving critical problems honestly and head on. They never take a check and move along.

The way we engaged with Miami Subs then is what we do with every company today: We figure out what is best for our clients, and then we provide it.

The lesson? Take care of the client, and your business will take care of itself.

It was like when I challenged my professor on that first day of business school all those years ago. I wasn't going to worry about anything but the goal, regardless of any other factor, because if I achieve the goal, everything else takes care of itself.

The franchisees in that room were more than receptive to our message and grateful for our honesty. They hired us with a $1.5 million contract. The safe play would have been to forget what we had seen in the stores and just sell them advertising. The safe play, yes—but the right play? The smart play? The best play? It would have been none of those things.

What Miami Subs needed—and what they really wanted—was an outside observer to come in and respect them enough to tell them the truth.

We took a risk, but it was the appropriate risk to take because we are committed to serving our clients the best way we can, and that must begin with looking at the so-called problem to see if it really is a problem. Chances are that finding the true obstacle to a client's success will require a little digging—going on site, getting your hands dirty, and doing more than just dragging out the same thing you did for a similar client the time before and the time before that.

Put down the cookie cutter.

More than a year later, Miami Subs had cleaned up every store. That enabled them to reap the benefits of the advertising we had produced, advertising that leveraged these newly clean and comfortable stores to bring in new customers and bring back old ones. Around that time I called up the president of the company to check in.

Average monthly sales were up for him 7 percent. Of course, I already knew that. It's my job to know. If I provide a service, I demand to know exactly how well it is working. Every detail matters: how much more a client is making, where they're up, what is driving the increase, and most important of all, how the advertising contributed to the new and bigger bottom line. Why bother? If you don't know exactly how you ended up where you are, you won't be able to do it again, and you won't be able to improve.

Here's the formula, top to bottom: Identify the real problem, keep track of how you approach it, and document your success. It's worth it every time.

By the way, this approach was even more radical than I've let on so far. Here's why: Most of the time, an advertising firm gets paid no matter what. The firm charges a fee, and if the ads work—that is, if they create more business—that's great for the client. If they don't, the agency still collects its fee.

Diabolical, isn't it? Doesn't matter if you create more business for a client or leave them in the cold, you still take home a check. Is it profitable? For a while, sure. But it also limits the success you make possible for yourself and your client.

Contrast that with my way of doing things: I was so confident in the power of candor that I reduced our fees for the work and agreed that we would make a profit only if Miami Subs did.

I bet *our* profit on *their* success. How about that?

What business would turn down an offer to work with an ad firm that does business my way? And what ad firm would make such a deal, except one that is utterly confident in its abilities?

Zimmerman is that firm, and that's why we're such a success.

We're leading the industry—dragging it kicking and screaming is more like it—toward the common-sense requirement that everything that comes out of our doors has to *create business for the client who paid for it.*

I have plenty of other examples. For instance, Fris Vodka Skandia hired us to launch a new vodka for them. We could have brainstormed some of our typical, attention-getting (and product-selling) ads and called it a day, but, as you know, that's not our style.

We are problem solvers, so the first thing we did was to thoroughly examine the situation and identify the real problem.

The Fris brand wasn't selling like it should. Our research team figured out pretty quickly that there was a deeper problem our new friends didn't know about—and it didn't have a thing to do with what was in the bottle.

Customers weren't ordering Fris vodka because they didn't want to embarrass themselves.

Why was that?

They didn't know how to say "Fris"!

Now, that's a problem that can be fixed, and we fixed it. We gave the product a tagline that told everybody how to pronounce the name: *Just say Fris—please.* It rhymes! (I'll bet a lot of you didn't know how to say "Fris" either, until you read that little catchphrase. See how this works?)

Clever. But did it work in the only way that matters? Did it add to their business?

With the tagline and our ad campaign in place in the first year, sales rose 40 percent.

So, *yeah*, it did work. With Fris, Miami Subs, and so many others, we showed our industry that there

can be more to this business than "pay your ad company, and hope it works."

When our clients make money, we make money.
That's a good deal for everybody, and it ought to be
what's expected on all sides. There can be no greater
motivation for an agency to do its best. We make our
bottom line dependent on theirs. Our success is a
function of how well we serve the people who pay us,
no more and no less.

This simple standard encourages people to work
hard and work smart toward a goal that matters, and
it creates a strong incentive to find the right goal in
the first place. It also creates a reason to measure effec-
tiveness at the end of the day in something other than
Cannes Lions and plaques on the wall.

It does something else too: It makes life a hell of a
lot tougher for those pointless agencies that just send a
bill every month and hope nobody notices that things
aren't getting any better for their clients. My agency is
the number-one agency in client profitability. There is
no more effective measure of success than that.

And that's fine with me.

Think about the people who rely on you. Are you
giving them what they need or just what you have

to offer? The achievers in life look for problems that need answers. They don't just look for problems they already have the answer *for*.

Consider your greatest ambition, your biggest goal, your wildest dream. Look deep at that challenge, and figure out what it is going to take to get there. Do whatever it takes, even when it's out of your comfort zone. *Especially* when it's out of your comfort zone.

Think beyond the ideas you have today. Work beyond your capacity right now. Stretch. Find the real problem and take it on.

JZ's CHAPTER TIPS

» When you start thinking like the people you're serving, your perspective broadens.

» Take care of the client, and your business will take care of itself.

» Identify the real problem, keep track of how you approach it, and document your success.

» Everything you provide a client must create business for the client.

» Do whatever it takes, even when it's out of your comfort zone—especially when it's out of your comfort zone.

GET AN EDUCATION,
OR GET A BROOM.

CHAPTER 27

When you ask people why they're going to school, most of them will tell you that they're earning a degree.

That was not my answer, because getting a diploma was never my most important goal. The point of education must be to *learn*. The degree is just a sign for the world to see that you have learned.

What I wanted to do professionally required a formal education, but what you want to do may not require a diploma at all. Still, every successful person must seek an education of some kind. When you pursue success, you have to acquire additional skills and new information. Most of the time that comes as formal education. There are exceptions: Steve Jobs and Bill Gates didn't complete college, but they studied a great deal on their own, and they had uniquely creative and disciplined minds. If you think that you don't need a formal education, think again. You probably need something—a certificate, a few classes, or, yes, a degree. But most people who say, "I'm smart enough to do without school," are just trying to get out of the hard work of learning.

I have had much success in life, but I guarantee that my success would not have been possible without an education. My education provided me with the necessary foundation to succeed in the world of business. I gained information, discipline, and the ability to think logically in every situation.

I thought I was pretty bright before I got to school, but I soon realized that there will always be more to learn. If you think you're the exception—that you don't need to spend time mastering the details of whatever it is you want to do, that you can learn it all on the job, or that you're smart enough to figure it out as you go—I guarantee you are going to quickly discover that you are wrong, and finding out will be a painful and likely humiliating lesson. For every college dropout who goes on to make a million bucks, there are hundreds more whose careers begin with big talk and end with cleaning up behind somebody else's elephants. Nobody's born smart. It has to be earned—and to be earned, it has to be learned.

Growing up in Old Bridge, New Jersey, made me want to leave Old Bridge, New Jersey. It wasn't a bad place; it was just that I wanted more. I knew there were only two ways out of the town I came from, sports or education. I was smart enough to realize that a career in sports was a long shot, or at the very best a short-term deal. Too much luck involved in that. But education! Now education carries you through a lifetime. The world can take your possessions, but it can never take away your education.

Trying to succeed without education is like trying to fly a jet without lessons. (Hell, if your goal is to be a pilot, it is trying to fly without lessons!) Education gives you the benefit of what other people have already figured out. Why reinvent the wheel?

As you learn, do more than just collect facts. Look for connections between what you're learning and what you already know. Say that you study for a big test and you get an A. You go on to the next subject, right?

Wrong!

The next step is to look for ways that new knowledge can get you closer to your intermediate and ultimate goals. Remember the key lesson from a few chapters ago: If you focus on learning something just for the test, you're focusing on output. But focus on learning it both for the test and your own goal, and you're focusing on outcome.

Some of you may feel that it is too late to go back to school. Wrong again. In one year's time you will be one year older, whether you spend that time watching cartoons or learning nuclear physics. In a year, you can have more education and be closer to your dream, or you can be exactly where you are right now.

When I was a kid, I wanted to be the best at everything, no matter what, and it bugged the hell out of me that there were kids smarter than I was. Yet that irritating truth led to an illuminating insight: There will always be people who are smarter than I am, but they will never have my work ethic, my drive, and my insane commitment.

I can't control how smart someone else is. But how hard I work? That's all mine. That's what has always set me apart from the sameness that defines the rest of the world. Some people will be smarter than me, but they will never outwork me.

One other thing: Education without a goal is a waste of effort. It's like acquiring a Ferrari and never taking it out of the garage. For your education to do you any good, you have to actually *do* something with it. No one's going to give you a prize for thinking deep thoughts and keeping them to yourself.

Finally, this—no matter how much knowledge you acquire, don't forget your common sense. You and I both know people who are "book smart" but who can't find their way out of a paper bag. Don't be like that. Similarly, don't imagine that your common sense is good enough without any formal learning to match. Common sense alone won't set you apart from the pack. That's why it's called common sense. You have to expand your intellectual holdings.

You wouldn't trust your health to an untrained doctor. You wouldn't trust your house to an untrained plumber or a do-it-yourself electrician (not unless you're curious to know what a house fire looks like). Why would you trust the most important thing in the world, your dream, to guesswork?

In the end, there's not much for the uneducated to

do beyond digging ditches and clearing tables. Even the kids behind the fast-food registers have to learn how to do what they do! Unless your future includes breaking rocks and washing cars, I suggest you get your ass to school and get your nose in a book.

JZ's CHAPTER TIPS

»   No one is born smart. Wisdom has to be earned—and to be earned, it has to be experienced.

»   Education gives you the benefit of what other people have already figured out.

»   I can't control how smart somebody else is. But how hard I work? That's all mine.

»   Education without a goal is a waste of effort.

»   No matter how much knowledge you acquire, hang on to your common sense.

»   Don't trust your future to your own uneducated guesses. Learn.

DID I HURT YOUR FEELINGS?
YOU'RE WELCOME.

CHAPTER 28

I'm lucky. I have made friends with a lot of interesting, accomplished, and occasionally famous people over the years, most of whom I met because we ended up working together. How did that happen? Turns out the people who believe that self-discipline and hard work are the only ways to the top end up in the same social circles. We attract each other. The best seek out the best.

One of those successful and interesting friends is Mark McNabb, chief operating officer of Volkswagen of America. When we met, he was an assistant regional manager of the northeast division of Nissan.

He worked his way up to general manager of Nissan America and then landed with Mercedes-Benz for a while, before deciding to return to Nissan America and Infiniti Worldwide. Next for Mark was a move to General Motors, specifically to oversee the Cadillac, Hummer, and Saab brands. Then he moved to serve as the president and CEO of Maserati North America and as the worldwide commercial director of Maserati S.p.A. As I mentioned, he is now with Volkswagen of America. Mark's experience is key here. He's a guy who knows cars, car buyers, and the car industry, inside and out. We were talking about his new position at Volkswagen, and he told me that he believed the famous Darth Vader spot (that's what we call a commercial in the advertising business) had really built up that brand.

Do you remember the Darth Vader spot? It aired in 2011, during Super Bowl XLV between the Packers and the Steelers. You probably remember a little boy in a Darth Vader mask waved a light saber, and lo and behold, the car in front of him started! "Don't you think it's a great spot, Jordan?" Mark asked me.

"No," I said. "I don't."

"No? What do you mean, *no*?" Mark said.

"I mean no, Mark. I don't think it's a great spot at

all." Then I explained to him my reasoning, based on nearly four decades of success in the advertising business. "Is it entertaining? Is it likeable? It sure is. But that's not the point of advertising," I said. "It's cute, but does it make you want to go buy a Volkswagen Passat? Did Volkswagen sell more cars after the spot aired, or did sales stay the same? Did Volkswagen sell more Passats in particular after the spot aired?"

Let's recap: Now, I'm talking to the new number two at Volkswagen, and I'm telling him that the pride-and-joy ad at his company isn't worth anything unless you can prove it's creating profit for the client.

Mark didn't miss a beat. "That's what I like about you, Jordan. Your perspective is so clear and so relevant."

There's the point. Successful people don't mince words. They don't modify or soften their opinion because the person who hears it might be offended. If people ask for your opinion, you can give them what you think they'd like to hear, or you can offer your true opinion. I knew Mark wanted my real opinion, not just some compliment. What good would that do? Mark McNabb doesn't need my encouragement. He doesn't need my compliments. And he certainly doesn't need my approval.

What he wants and needs is the honest opinion of people just as committed to quality as he is. Clarity. Relevance. Honesty. When successful people speak, that's what you get.

If you want to be successful, acquire an unflagging commitment to candor. That's not to say you should set out to insult people or be provocative for its own sake. But when someone asks your professional opinion, give that person your *informed and honest* point of view, even if it's uncomfortable to do so. In business, that's called doing *due diligence*. What they do with your advice is up to them, but you've fulfilled the obligation of a true professional by providing your best professional assessment.

Alternatively, if you don't know anything about the subject, don't guess. Be honest: Tell them that you haven't read enough about the subject to have an informed opinion.

You think knowing the answer impresses people? Admitting that you don't know the answer is just as impressive—and just as valuable. Why? Because so few people have the guts to admit when they don't know!

Answer without knowing what you're talking about, and sooner or later you'll get caught in a pretty uncomfortable position. I once saw a funny piece on late-night TV, on *Jimmy Kimmel Live*. A reporter for the show went up and down Hollywood Boulevard asking people what they thought of the previous night's episode of *Dancing with the Stars*. Nearly every person they stopped—young, old, male, female—described the amazing dancing they had seen and how much they had enjoyed it.

The thing is, *Dancing* hadn't been on TV at all. Every person who answered just made up what they thought the reporter wanted to hear. But it wasn't the reporter who ended up looking foolish. It was the person who didn't know what he was talking about, but who acted as if he did.

If you want to be successful, speak your informed and honest mind. All you can offer is what you know and understand. Anything else is a waste of your time and everyone else's.

JZ's CHAPTER TIPS

» Successful people don't mince words.

» If someone asks for your opinion, tell the truth. Acquire an unflagging commitment to candor.

» If you don't know the answer, don't guess.

» If you make up answers, you will eventually be exposed.

» If you want to be successful, speak your informed and honest mind. All you can offer is what you know and understand. Anything else is a waste of your time and everyone else's.

HOW *NOT* TO LIVE YOUR LIFE *OR* LEADING FEARLESSLY VERSUS FOLLOWING FEARFULLY.

CHAPTER 29

I can tell you all day long how to succeed. I can lay out the plan and give you encouragement and show you examples from my own life and from history. But that's not how everybody learns.

Some people learn best when they hear about what's wrong and then recognize it in their own lives. For some of you, that's the only way to get your attention. So at this point I'm going to turn this whole thing upside down. I'm going to stop telling you how to lead fearlessly, and instead, I'll tell you how to follow fearfully!

Following Fearfully!
How to avoid hard work,
Miss out on your dreams,
Stay in the rut you're in,
And get defeated by the roadblocks
That keep you from achieving
the success you deserve.

1 **Don't worry about education.** Talk about over-rated! Just bluff your way through things. That's what all the "smart" guys do.

2 **Make it up as you go along.** You don't need a plan. Planning is for losers. Even though every great thing ever achieved in history was built on careful thinking in advance, you are the exception. You're best as a fly-by-the-seat-of-the-pants gal. Go for it!

3 **If you're in a job you hate, stay there.** Life is supposed to be boring and difficult. Get used to it. The smart play is to find something familiar and never stray from it. So what if you're unhappy? Who cares if you want something else out of life? You can't do a damn thing about your own circumstances, and there's always a perfectly good reason

to stay in the sorry situation you're in. Always settle for second best!

4 **Complain all the time, and don't do anything about it.** Who among us hasn't spent an unforgettable and uplifting evening with someone who hates his life and has to tell you all about it? You know the kind of person I'm talking about, the one who is always full of one-of-these-days stories that never quite come true. As you know, these are the kind of people everybody loves to be around. Make yourself just like them: Complain constantly to anyone who will listen, and never, ever try to change your situation.

5 **Don't dig too deep into the lives of your heroes.** If it looks like someone has money and success, that's good enough for it to rub off on you. Appearance is all that matters. Don't worry about learning what they did to get there—and never approach them personally to ask a question! Everything you need to know about successful people can be learned by gazing at them admiringly and making a jealous wish.

6 **Tear down other people.** You can't win unless someone else loses, right? The more negativity and distrust you spread along the way, the faster you'll

get to the top and the more room there will be when you get there! Cut loose the dead weight. Use 'em and lose 'em.

7   **Surround yourself with second-rate people.** Don't you want to always be the smartest one in the room? Of course you do! And you sure don't need a bunch of egghead show-offs around, making you feel like a dummy. The more losers you put around you, the more obvious your genius will be!

8   **Remember that teamwork never solved any-thing.** If memory serves—now I could be wrong here, but I don't think so—we talk about a "man" on the moon, not "men" on the moon. It didn't take a team of people to get there, just a guy sitting on top of a rocket giving orders. Anything you want to do in life you can do by yourself. You don't need the expertise of others. And you certainly don't need to cooperate with a bunch of so-called experts. All they want is a piece of your action.

9   **Do just enough to get by.** You know how it goes for the losers in life. They deliver more than they ever promised, they deliver it faster than they prom-ised, and the quality is better than they promised.

Talk about wasted effort! All they had to do was deliver something—anything—then go home and play *Call of Duty*. Time spent on quality and efficiency is time you could have spent on yourself. Let the other guy work late into the night for his success. On the race to the top, "good enough" is good enough for you.

10 **Treat yourself like a king early and often.** Don't spend your time getting ahead, and don't save your money for your big goals. Have fun right now! Live it up, and let tomorrow take care of itself. Thank goodness you don't have some foolish plan to slow you down. Otherwise, you might think it's the smart move to save your money or put in extra time to improve yourself. Successful people live it up 24/7, right? Be like them! Spend your energy on immediate pleasures that last only a minute.

11 **Remember that competition never helped anybody.** If there are already other people doing what you want to do, there's probably no room for you to join. Give up. Every game is rigged, and the only people who win are born into it or lucky or cheaters—probably all of the above.

12 **If you can't start at the top, don't start at all.** Successful people never lower themselves to do any job other than other than that of boss. There is nothing to be learned from doing even the lowest job in the company. The head of Zimmerman Advertising started out doing everything in the office, right down to sweeping the floor. What a sucker he is!

13 **Suffering and sacrifice are the world's way of telling you that you're doing it wrong.** If you've ever worked out, you've probably heard somebody say that pain is just weakness on its way out of the body. Not true! When you feel pain—and by that I mean any kind of discomfort at all, from being a little sleepy to being bored—take that as a signal to give up. Find something easier to do. Something that's a struggle is never worth it.

14 **Always have an excuse.** It's so much easier to blame somebody or something else than to do the hard work yourself. You don't even have to make up excuses on your own, because I'm going to do it for you! Here are some excuses you can use:

- You didn't give me enough information/money.

- I didn't have the right tools.

- I'm surrounded by idiots.

- I was busy doing something else.

- You didn't give me enough time.

- You must have misunderstood.

- It'll be worth the wait.

- You don't need it anyway.

- This is too complicated in the first place.

And the best of all,

- It's not my fault.

15 **Always remember that experience has no lessons to teach.** They call it the past for a reason: It's over. There is nothing to be learned from someone who lived ten or a hundred or a thousand years ago. Times have changed! We have computers now! There's not even anything to learn from someone who's out there today, because that person isn't you. Experience is for suckers. Your own instinct is all you'll ever need to get ahead of all those hard-working schmucks.

16 **It's all about luck.** Let's face it, the only people who win are the ones who happened to be in the right place at the right time. You're either an overnight

success, or you're a failure. Whoever heard of somebody spending years in school learning a craft, then putting in more time as an apprentice, actually doing something alongside someone with real know-how, then launching a business or setting out toward a goal and sacrificing day after day, year after year, relying on hard work to get the things he or she wants in life? That never happens. Successful people are born, not made. They just get lucky.

17 **Never forget that the world owes you a living.** After all, you didn't ask to be here. Your attitude should demonstrate to people that you're not there to serve them, they are there to serve you.

18 **If you have a great idea and somebody disagrees, give in.** They're saving you a lot of heartache. After all, the great advances in human history all came from people who listened to the naysayers, right?

19 **Ignore advice from your so-called superiors.** People in charge usually reached that position the same way you intend to, by floating through life hoping that something good would just fall out of the sky. What could they possibly know? Remember Dean Wormer from *Animal House*? He said, "Fat, drunk,

and stupid is no way to go through life." What a jerk he was! And he was wrong anyway! Think of all the fat, drunk, and stupid success stories out there! Why, the world is just teeming with fat, drunk, and stupid millionaires, athletes, singers, actors, and superstars! I'll bet you're next!

20 **You don't have to be the best at what you do, not really.** Think about your favorite sports team. You don't care if your players hustle for the ball, do you? You're just there to see them run around. You probably don't care if your team recruits the best players, either, as long as everybody's having fun. It's like when you get your car worked on. You don't care if the mechanic is any good, as long as he looks busy. He's surely doing his best, and that's good enough, whether the car gets fixed or not. Right?

There you have it, twenty rules for "following fearfully." If you see yourself doing any of these, stop.

THE SAYINGS OF CHAIRMAN Z.

CHAPTER 30

Here we are, the end of the line. But if you've come this far, maybe you're willing to come a little further.

I want you to succeed in the relentless pursuit of your goals as much as I want to succeed in my own. I have been fortunate in my life to have discovered the path to success.

Now it's your turn.

Are you the next Steve Jobs, or the twenty-first century's Henry Ford? You might be, if that's what you want—if you aim high. Your success could even be a link in the chain of someone else's great achievement. Successful people create new products and ideas, new goods and services, and new playgrounds of opportunity for the rest of us, so the possibilities are literally endless.

From the young woman who wants to open a nail salon to the young man who wants to become a manager, from the couple who wants to open a bed and breakfast to the young professional who wants to find his place higher up that corporate ladder and to the kid who wants to go to the college of his dreams—whoever you are and whatever you want to achieve, what I have just described is the way to get there. It's worth doing, and no matter how intimidated you are by life, know this: *Your life matters*. Don't waste any more of it.

I'll wrap up my book with a summary of the advice you've just read, boiled down so you can glance at it when you need some inspiration or when you just want to look back with a little pride on how far you've come. So—some thoughts for your journey.

JZ on Finding the Path to Success

- Be insanely committed to your own life. Be dedicated, committed, unrelenting, unfailing, unstoppable.

- Find your passion. Find something that you are so passionate about that you want it to be part of every single day and to play an important role in your life. Don't ask how much money it will earn you or how hard it might be to achieve. Just go for it.

- When it comes to planning your life, put down the cookie cutter.

- Be insane enough to walk through hell to do whatever you dream.

- Differentiate yourself. Don't drown in the sea of sameness.

- Our nation was not built on mediocrity. Your own bright future will not be built on mediocrity, either.

- You define your brand, and your brand defines you.

- You'll never *get* where you're going if you don't know *where* you're going.

- A lot of people may be smarter than you are. That's okay, as long as you outwork them.

JZ on Staying on Top

- Do whatever it takes.

- If you're insanely committed to the truth, you don't care who delivers it, a PhD or a kid in his first day of class.

- No matter how much knowledge you acquire in your field of expertise, hang on to your street smarts, and remember your common sense.

- If you don't have a goal, get one.

- Work beyond the capacity you think you have. Exceed your own expectations. Exceed the expectations of others.

- It's the touchdown that matters, not how pretty the pass is.

- We are what we repeatedly do.

JZ on Avoiding Regret

- It may be too late for you to start early, but it's never too late to start.

- If you wake up every morning feeling like *there has to be more to life than this*, it's probably because you never identified what you want to achieve in your life, what your goals are, or what you are passionate about. Chose a goal and commit to achieve it.

- If you don't choose to pursue the things you say you love, you can be sure that you didn't love them in the first place.

- Follow the path that leads to what you really want, no matter the pain. Ignore the pain.

- Heartache and discontent come along in life most often because it's easier to be the one life happens to than the one who makes life happen.

- Take charge of your life right now. Don't be one of those people who later in life says, *I wish I would have . . . I know I could have . . .*

JZ on Self-Motivation

- Success isn't about where you start out. It's about where you're going and what you're willing to sacrifice to get there.

- If you don't have the success you want, it's your fault and nobody else's.

- Life is a series of choices. For each one, you choose to sacrifice toward your goal or you decide to put it off.

- There is nothing in the world you can't achieve, if you are willing to work hard to get it.

- You never know where the next great idea is going to come from, so keep yourself open.

- Believe in yourself and what you know is true, and don't let anybody drive you off course.

JZ on Business

- Outcome beats output every single time. Outcome is your goal. In the real world, nobody gets paid for just showing up.

- There's plenty of room at the top, and plenty of business to go around once you get there, but, first, you have to get there.

- Success is driven by competition, and competition is the key to quality. Be insanely committed to competition.

- More often than you know, the big wheels in life started as little gears.

- Don't carry your personal business into work. Leave home at home.

- People who depend on you don't care much for how pretty your effort is. What matters is the bottom line.

- When you start thinking like the people you're serving, your perspective changes for the better.

- Last time I checked, my bank sent me a statement accounting for dollars and cents, not trophies and plaques.

- There's only one opinion that matters other than my own: that of my client.

JZ on Education

- The point of education is to *learn*. The degree is just a sign for the world to see that you *have* learned and that you have proven your commitment and earned a degree.

- Don't imagine that your diploma entitles you to a damn thing.

- A lack of education leaves you with few options and limited opportunities.

- If you don't know the answer, don't pretend you do.

- You will not be getting out of school on the day you graduate. You will be entering The School of Life.

JZ on Sacrifice

- To achieve a dream tomorrow, do without things today. Focus on the long-term goal, and recognize the intermediate prizes are exactly that—intermediate.

- Your will and your self are your birthrights. Everything else? That's up to you.

- You either man up, or you don't.

JZ on Failure and Fear

- Fear is fuel.

- You're going to make mistakes, probably some big ones. But *failure to reach your goal* is not an option.

- The reticular activating system programs your brain to filter negativity and discard it. Make use of it.

- Mike Tyson had it right when he said, "Everybody has a plan until he gets punched in the mouth." Be ready to react, regroup, and change as needed.

- Your goal is not to impress your friends but to impress yourself.

JZ on Habits of the Successful

- Successful people focus relentlessly on the big goal, the greater truth, the point down the road that they are determined to reach.

- Successful people are concerned with solving problems, not just collecting a check and moving on.

- Personal-life excuses are the sorriest excuses there are.

- Successful people are candid.

- Your reputation is your greatest asset.

- There is deep value in deep understanding.

- A true visionary doesn't settle for anything less than transformation. Vision is seeing what could be.

- You either keep going or you quit.

- Steve Jobs once told a group of graduates to "Stay hungry. Stay foolish." I'll add one more thing: Stay desperate.

- Don't give up. Henry Ford, Walt Disney, and George Foreman all went bankrupt before they made their fortunes.

- Life isn't fair. So what?

That's it! Now it's time to put what you've learned here into action. If you've taken my story to heart, you're already on your way.

Good luck. Now get busy.

You sleep when *you die*.

And always remember: Relentlessly pursue the goal, but never rest in the glory.

INDEX

A

addiction to you, clients',
    68–70
advertising agency with client
    focus, 23–25, 39–41,
    111, 178, 211–15,
    216–17. *See also*
    Zimmerman Advertising
advertising industry
    and client profitability, 24,
        111, 220
    Darth Vader spot, 232–33
    fees for ads, 217–18
    Hollywood movie analogy,
        38–39
    Lion trophy, 174–78
    Zimmerman as
        controversial within,
        173–75
America and American
    exceptionalism, 181–84
Aquino, Judith, 70–71
arrogance, 85–88, 90
autocracies, 55–56
awareness, 1–3

B

being the best
    about, 151–52
    doing whatever it takes,
        41–42
    insane commitment to,
        42, 43
    mastering required skills,
        37–38, 39–40, 41
    and professionalism, 59
    work ethic for, 3, 139,
        151–52, 220,
        226–27
    Zimmerman Advertising
        techniques, 38–41
Biggest Loser, The (TV
    program), 143
Bossypants (Fey), 64
brain surgery, on yourself,
    109–11, 112
brand awareness, 196
brandtailing, 211–12
bullshitters
    about, 97–98, 102
    self-made people vs.,
        98–99, 100–101

bullshitters (*continued*)
  test for identifying,
    99–100
Burns, Ursula, 70
business, 23, 252–53

C

candor, 15, 20–23, 234–35
Cannes Lions International
    Festival of Creativity,
    174–78
change
  and overcoming fear,
    129–31
  progress via little
    improvements,
    103–4, 107–8
  transformational change,
    104–7, 108
character and professionalism,
    63–64
character, building your,
    195–98
choices
  and desperation, 160
  fight or flight, 125
  path to what you really
    want, 2–3, 4–5, 93,
    204–5, 208
  and personal brand,
    197–98
  productivity vs. the easy
    thing, 61, 206–7
  rejecting negative
    thoughts, 127–30

  sacrifice vs. immediate
    gratification, 32
Churchill, Winston, 73, 123
clients
  about, 117, 118
  addiction to you, 68–70
  insane commitment to, 67,
    68–72, 73, 79, 221
  reasons for hiring you,
    115–16, 117
  success of, 137, 176, 179,
    217, 219–20
  thinking like, 210–11
  turning down controlling
    clients, 116–17
  Zimmerman Advertising's
    focus on clients,
    23–25, 39–41,
    111, 178, 211–15,
    216–17, 219
college as first big decision, 2.
    See also education
commitment. *See* insane
    commitment
common sense, 227
competition
  about, 46–48, 56, 58
  cultural view of, 48–49,
    53–54
  and exercise, 45–46
  free enterprise vs.
    autocracies, 48,
    55–56, 181–84
  as performance-based
    metric, 150–51

competition (*continued*)
and professionalism, 64
as quality control, 50–53
and success in life, 49–50,
53, 54–55
Trophy Generation vs.,
145–46, 150
complaints, 239
controversial nature, 174,
176–78
Cuba, 55–56
cultural view of competition,
48–49, 53–54
cycle of defeat, 119–21,
138–39

D

Darth Vader spot, 232–33
delegating, 88–89
desperation, 157–59, 160,
161
discipline, 95
Disney, Walt, 157–58
distractions and temptations,
23, 166, 169–70, 173,
179
DMV, 50, 51
doing the right thing
about, 26
for clients, 116–17
fulfilling promises, 24, 65,
67–68, 79
honesty with clients,
212–15, 216–17,
233–35, 236

professionalism as, 61–62
speaking up for what's
right, 18–21
See also professionalism
dreams, 33, 34–35, 62, 181–
84, 188. *See also* goals
due diligence, 234–35
Dylan, Bob, 117

E

Edison, Thomas, 187
education
about, 14, 197, 253–54
forming a personal brand
in high school,
195–98
goals for, 227
importance of, 93, 95,
223–25, 227–28
learning about goals,
203–4
successful dropouts, 156,
225
ZAP at USF, 22
Zimmerman at USF,
11–12, 15, 17–22,
27, 215–16
ego, 85–88, 90, 155
employees, 88–89
entitlement mentality, 149,
244. *See also* Trophy
Generation
excellence, 198
exceptionalism, American,
181–84

excuses
    about, 77–78, 83, 242–43
    as bullshit, 1, 3–4
    fear, 126
    no excuses philosophy,
        78–80
    personal problems and
        IDFC, 80–82
    time as, 3
    for Trophy Generation,
        145
    whatever it takes attitude
        vs., 9, 67, 72, 151,
        221
exercise, 45–46

F
failure
    about, 124, 254–55
    in childhood, 144
    cycle of defeat, 119–21,
        138–39
    "failure is not an option" as
        state of mind, 119,
        123–24
    from losing touch with
        your goal, 169–70
    possibility of vs. certainty
        of, 129–31
    restructuring failing
        business, 185–86
    value of, 55, 121–23,
        135–39
    and wealth, 205–6
fast-food restaurants, 51

fear as fuel
    about, 132, 254–55
    for change, 129–31
    fight choice, 125–27, 129
    flight choice, 125
    recession, 130–31
    rejecting negative
        thoughts, 127–30
    for Trophy Generation,
        158
fearful following vs. fearless
    leading, 238–45
FedEx, 52
Fey, Tina, 64
fight or flight choice, 125
focus, single-minded, 165–67,
    209–11
Ford, Henry, 104–5, 106–7,
    157–58
Foreman, George, 157–58
free enterprise, 48, 55–56,
    181–84
Fris Vodka Skandia, 218–20

G
Gates, Bill, 156, 160, 224
goals
    about, 171
    achieving your goals,
        41–42, 43, 126–27
    choosing productivity, 62
    doing whatever it takes,
        221, 222
    dreaming big, 33, 34–35
    educational, 227

goals (*continued*)
  importance of, 203–4,
    205–7, 208
  and inspiration of
    desperation, 158–59
  intermediate achievements,
    14, 167–70, 226
  and no excuses
    philosophy, 81–82
  passion for, 198–99
  sacrificing for goals vs.
    acceptance of less, 2,
    4, 27, 30–33, 35
  single-minded focus on,
    165–67, 209–11
  See also dreams
Great Recession, 130–31

H
habits, creation of, 5, 197–98
happiness, 54, 93, 182, 204–5
happy talk, 97–98
honesty, 212–15, 216–17,
    233–35, 236
human nature
  accepting good enough, 60
  attracting similar
    personalities, 231
  competition, 46
  and inspiration of
    desperation, 158–59
  real you disguised, 193–94
humble beginning, 91
hype transplants, 100

I
IDFC (I don't effing care),
    80–82
incremental improvements,
    104–7, 108
insane commitment
  to candor, 15, 20–23,
    234–35
  to competition, 54–55
  learning about, 11
  to people who rely on you,
    67, 68–72, 73, 79,
    221
  to suffering for your goal
    and sacrificing to get
    there, 27, 30–33, 35
  to your own life, 11–13,
    15–16, 131–32
  See also being the best;
    doing the right thing;
    professionalism
insanity, 9–10
inspiration of desperation,
    157–59, 160, 161
intention, 167. *See also* goals
intermediate achievements,
    14, 167–70, 226
internships, 70–72

J
Jimmy Kimmel Live (TV
    program), 235
Jobs, Steve, 71, 156, 160, 224
Johnson, Betsey, 71

"Just Say No" campaign, 11–12

L

Lane Bryant, 122–23
leadership
    following fearfully vs.,
        238–45
    leading fearlessly, 237
    as understanding skills of
        others, 88–89
learning, 224–26. *See also*
    education
learning from mistakes,
    135–39
letters from teachers for
    getting into college,
    196–97
lies vs. truth, 152
Lion trophy, 174–78
loving what you do, 2, 3–5,
    31–32, 198–99
luck, 244

M

McNabb, Mark, 231–33
metrics
    as basis for ad agency
        success, 23–24
    client success, 137, 176,
        179, 217, 219–20
    competition as
        performance-based
        metric, 150–51
Miami Subs, 212–15, 216–17,

218
mistakes
    about, 133
    beating yourself up for
        (not), 133–35
    learning from, 135–39
Mitsubishi, 121, 136–38, 139
Monaghan, Tom, 157–58
Morgan, J.P., 185–87

N

National Institute on Drug
    Abuse (NIDA), 11–12
Nissan North America, 122
North Korea, 56

O

obligations, 4
obstacles, 72–73, 129
oil industry, 106–7
opportunities, obstacles as,
    72–73
optimism vs. pessimism,
    130–31
outcome over output
    about, 173, 180
    focus on outcome, 167–70
    identifying desired
        outcome, 166–67
    and learning, 225–26
    Lion trophy vs., 174–78
    at Zimmerman
        Advertising, 39–41
    See also goals

output, 168–70, 176–78. *See also* outcome over output
overachievers, 184–89, 191

P

paper route, 10–11, 67–68
passion, 94–96, 198–99
perceptions of others about you, 196
perseverance, 123–24
personal brand
about, 194–95
decisions leading to, 198–99, 200
forming in high school, 195–98
personalities, 193–94
personal problems, 80–82
perspective and goal achievement, 167–70
pessimism vs. optimism, 130–31
power of your thoughts
beating yourself up for mistakes, 134
decisions leading to passion, 198–99
overcoming fear, 127–30
single-minded focus on your goal, 165–67
on your brain, 109–11, 112, 119–20
pride as obstacles in your mind, 85–88, 90
priorities vs. excuses, 79

problem solving, 209–11
productivity vs. doing the easy thing, 61, 206–7
professionalism
about, 59–60, 66
character and, 63–64
choosing productivity as, 60–63
as doing the right thing, 61–62
reputation building, 64–65
profit, importance of, 18–21, 22–23, 28, 177–79
Pulp Fiction (movie), 63
purchase funnel, 18–21
Pursuit of Happyness, The (movie), 71

Q

quality control, competition as, 50–53

R

railroad industry, 185
real you, 193–94, 198. *See also* personal brand
recession, 130–31
regret, avoiding, 250–51
reputation building, 64–65
restructuring failing business, 185–86
results-driven advertising agency, 24, 39, 40–41, 111, 178. *See also* Zimmerman Advertising

reticular activating system
(RAS), 109–11, 112
Rockefeller, John D., 187
Roosevelt, Theodore "Teddy,"
190
Rose, Pete, 134–35

S

sacrifice
about, 254
for achieving goals vs.
acceptance of less, 2,
4, 27, 30–33, 35
immediate gratification
vs., 32
motto for, 31–32
self-esteem, 54, 57
self-made people, 98–99,
100–101
self-motivation, 251–52
self-reflection, 189–90
skills, mastering, 37–38,
39–40, 41
small change, 103–4, 107–8
Sorkin, Andrew Ross, 70–71
Soviet Union, 55
Spielberg, Steven, 70
sports teams, 245
steamboats, 184–85
strengths, identifying, 41–42,
43
success
about, 247–50
and choices, 198–99, 200
choosing productivity, 62

of clients, 137, 176, 179,
217, 219–20
and competition, 49–50, 53
as courage to continue,
123
with honesty, 212–15,
216–17, 233–35,
236
and no excuses
philosophy, 80,
81–82
of overachievers, 184–89,
191
and passion for goals, 68,
72, 198–99
pride vs., 85–88, 90
in spite of unfairness, 91,
96, 123
and triumph over fear, 129
whatever it takes attitude,
9, 67, 72, 151, 221
successful people, habits of,
255–56
suffering for your goal and
sacrificing to get there,
27, 30–33, 35
superiority, 85–88, 90

T

temptations and distractions,
23, 166, 169–70, 173,
179
thoughts. *See* power of your
thoughts
Timmy Tomorrow, 99–100

tough times, 159
transformational change,
    104–7, 108
trophies
    earning, 147
    a Lion, 174–78
    as quick and easy victory,
        179
Trophy Generation
    about, 143–45, 153
    breaking away from, 149,
        150–52
    as entitlement mentality,
        149, 244
    reality vs., 145–47,
        149–50
    winners and losers vs.,
        144–46
trusting yourself, 115–18
turnaround artists, 185–86
"12 Successful People Who
    Started as Interns"
    (Aquino), 70–71
Tyson, Mike, 123

U

unhappiness, 93, 204–5
United States Postal Service,
    51–53
University of South Florida
    (USF), 11–12, 15,
    17–22, 27, 215–16
U.S. Steel, 186

V

Vanderbilt, Cornelius, 184–85
vanity, moving beyond, 86
vision, 190
visionary change, 104–7, 108

W

wealth, 205–6
whatever it takes attitude, 9,
    67, 72, 151, 221
winners and losers, 144–46.
    See instead Trophy
    Generation
wisdom, 118, 229
work ethic, 3, 139, 151–52,
    220, 226–27

Z

Zimmerman Advertising
    about, 23–25, 38–39
    being the best, 38–41
    client focus, 23–25, 39–41,
        111, 178, 211–15,
        216–17, 219
    clients' success, 137, 176,
        179, 217, 219–20
    corporate headquarters,
        33–34
    first office, 28–30, 33
    metrics as basis for, 23–24
    no excuses philosophy,
        78–79
    outcome over output,
        39–41

Zimmerman Advertising
(continued)
plans for, 27–28
Zimmerman's early jobs in,
85, 87–88
Zimmerman Advertising
Program (ZAP) at USF, 22
Zimmerman, Jordan
childhood, 9–11, 91–95,
195–96, 225
early jobs at Zimmerman
Advertising, 85,
87–88

job hunting after college,
12–14
"Just Say No" campaign,
11–12
paper route, 10–11, 67–68
sayings of, 248–56
University of South
Florida, 11–12, 15
Zuckerberg, Mark, 156, 160

Jordan Zimmerman is founder and chairman of Zimmerman Advertising, headquartered in Ft. Lauderdale, Florida. The Zimmerman Advertising powerhouse is the fourteenth largest ranked advertising agency in the world with published billings in excess of $3 billion. Originally founding his company as "the first metrics-driven business solutions firm that happened to do advertising," Jordan has become known as "Advertising's Bad Boy" and trademarked his own term Brandtailing,™ a well-known methodology throughout the industry. More than 1,100 associates in twenty-two offices live by his motto "Relentlessly pursue the client's goal, but never rest in the glory."

Jordan is involved in several charitable organizations and not-for-profit educational institutions, and has received numerous awards for his generosity and philanthropy to the greater community. Jordan and his wife reside with their children in Boca Raton, Florida.